Spicing Up the Cariboo

Canadian Mental
Health Association
Cariboo Chilcotin
Mental health for all

01 02 03 04 05 17 16 15 14 13

Caitlin Press Inc.
8100 Alderwood Road
Halfmoon Bay, BC V0N 1Y1
www.caitlin-press.com

Edited by Patricia Wolfe.
Text and cover design by Vici Johnstone.
Cover artwork by Cathie Allen.
Printed in Canada

Caitlin Press Inc. acknowledges financial support from the Government of Canada through the Canada Book Fund and the Canada Council for the Arts, and from the Province of British Columbia through the British Columbia Arts Council and the Book Publisher's Tax Credit.

Canada Council
for the Arts

Conseil des Arts
du Canada

BRITISH COLUMBIA
ARTS COUNCIL

Library and Archives Canada Cataloguing in Publication

Spicing Up the Cariboo: characters, cultures & cuisines of the Cariboo

Chilcotin / Margaret-Anne Enders, Thomas Lee Salley, Marilyn Livingston.

ISBN 978-1-927575-10-9

1. Cooking. 2. Cultural pluralism—British Columbia—Cariboo Region.

3. Cariboo Region (B.C.)—Biography. 4. Cookbooks. I. Enders, Margaret-Anne,

1969- II. Salley, Thomas Lee, 1951- III. Livingston, Marilyn, 1959-

TX714.S653 2013   641.5   C2013-901037-8

Spicing Up the Cariboo

Characters,
Cultures & Cuisines
of the Cariboo Chilcotin

Margaret-Anne Enders, Marilyn Livingston,
and Tom Salley, with Bettina Schoen

Introduction by Christian Petersen
Foreword by Sage Birchwater

CAITLIN PRESS

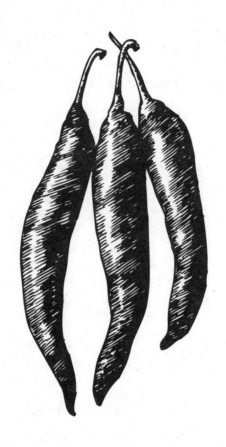

For Kelly, Lucas and Jamie—the spice of my life.

—Margaret-Anne Enders

For my mom, Margaret Livingston, Aunt Ethel Stanford, Aunt Hazel Nish and my Grandmother Ady. When I think of these beautiful ladies who blessed my life, my memories are filled with love, family meals and delicious food. And thank you, Clay, for keeping the home fires burning.

—Marilyn Livingston

I would like to dedicate this book to my fellow immigrants and to all those who endeavour to make this a greener world. Together we are building a happier, healthy community. Thank you.

—Tom Salley

I am dedicating Spicing Up the Cariboo to all my wonderful friends here. Thanks for the many fabulous meals we shared and for making the Cariboo my home.

—Bettina Schoen

Contents

Tastes of Europe

Tastes of Asia

Tastes of Australia, South Africa and Fiji

Introduction

Memorable Meals
& Stories

Meals are made memorable for many reasons, the company, the ambiance and occasion, and the food itself. Most often it is those we break bread with, family and friends, and the relationships between us, that bring the added colour, scents, flavours, and emotion to the memory. Traditional ethnic dishes are often at the heart of customs and provide much of the identity of a culture, for those who partake as well as the wider community.

From the memories, the relationships, the customs and cultures, our personal stories are created. So in a genuine sense the food feeds the narratives.

Reading the stories and recipes contributed for this collection was a pleasure and a privilege. It brought home to me a number of values shared by those involved, and I will note just a few. First, what a diverse and mosaic culture we live in, enriched by older cultures from around the world. There is no typical Canadian, thanks be to all, and we see that fact affirmed here in the Cariboo. Second, food is fun and food is tasty, delicious, nutritious and literally empowering. There is no end to the flavours, textures, colours, no end to what we can learn about food in all its forms, and no end to what we can learn from others in the course of kitchen conversations.

Another value that the stories in this collection confirm is how truly fortunate we are to live where we do, in Canada, and right here in the region of the Cariboo Chilcotin. We may meet and greet at the grocery store, the Cariboo Growers Co-op, the Oliver Street market, the Harvest Fair, or at a pancake breakfast during the Stampede. It often goes unsaid, but this is a great place to live. And the fact that this project came to fruition speaks well of our community. The contributors' personal stories tell us why their families chose to come to Canada, and to the Cariboo, and in a very real way remind us of the broader rights and freedoms we all treasure.

Spicing Up the Cariboo includes offerings from forty-nine contributors, representing more than forty cultures. These recipes are varied and wonderful. I was asked to review them based upon my experience as a professional cook, and I want to note that I made very few suggestions. The main reason is that they are excellent as they are. A second reason is that I never read any recipe as though it is written in stone. Most of us like cilantro, but apparently some do not. For my taste, I often double the suggested amount of garlic or throw in a sprig of fresh thyme or rosemary from the herb garden, or a habanero from the pepper patch.

A number of these dishes are brand new to me, and I look forward to experiencing their flavours and form. Many sound mouth watering. The papa rellena from Peru, the Laotian beef salad and the pirukad from Estonia are all starred on my to-do list. And no matter how many cookbooks you may have on your shelf already, it is unlikely that any of those contain a recipe for moose tripe.

So, welcome to our table. May the stories nourish understanding, and the meals feed new friendships. This collection holds much in store, dear reader. Enjoy!

—Christian Petersen

Foreword

Williams Lake has often been passed off as a rough and ready sawmill and cow town, and its people pegged in the broad stereotype of cultural sameness, like the featureless lodgepole pine forests that blanket the landscape.

But beneath the surface, like the rich biodiversity that is so much a part of the Cariboo Chilcotin region, the citizens of Williams Lake are a surprisingly rich multicultural mix. This book will attest to that.

My task in this book's creation was to help edit the stories collected by Tom Salley, Marilyn Livingston and Margaret-Anne Enders. I confess that oral history is one of my sweet joys as a writer in this region. Every one of us has a story, and each of us comes from somewhere unique, bringing the essence of our background and traditions with us. Nothing better reflects who we are than the food we eat.

What totally surprised me was the extent of cultural diversity that exists in this region.

These pages contain the stories and recipes of forty-nine families and individuals who trace their roots to forty-five distinct cultural backgrounds that circle the globe.

In the true Canadian sense, gauged by the palate of its citizens, Williams Lake is a multicultural community.

The following list shows the breadth of ethnic origins reflected in the stories and recipes of this book: American Cowboy Culture, Australian, Bangladeshi, Belgian (Flemish), Bermudan, Brazilian, British, Chinese, Czech, Dakelh (Southern Carrier), Danish, Estonian, Fijian, Filipino, French Canadian, German, Greek, Honduran, Italian, Irish, Japanese, Jewish, Korean, Laotian, Lenapean, Lithuanian, Mexican, New England Colonist, Norwegian, Pakistani, Peruvian, Polish, Portuguese, Punjabi,

Romanian, Scottish, Secwepemc (Shuswap), Sioux, South African, Sri Lankan, Swedish, Swiss, Thai, Tsilhqot'in and Ukrainian.

Of course, this book doesn't claim to represent all the ethnic backgrounds and cultures found in the region, but it does give you a taste of its complexity.

It is interesting that we have three of the Cariboo Chilcotin's aboriginal cultures represented in these pages: the Dakelh (Southern Carrier) of Anahim Lake, the Tsilhqot'in of the Chilcotin Plateau and the Secwepemc (Shuswap) of the Cariboo east of the Fraser River. Combined, they give us a tiny hint of how indigenous cultures utilize the native plants, animals and fish of this region to survive.

Several of the interviewees come from a mix of cultural backgrounds, and some families consciously celebrate two or more ethnic traditions. Sometimes recipes are melded in interesting ways that reflect a cultural mix. For instance, Greek food prepared with an Italian flair.

Others share the food traditions they have adopted from other places around the world. And that is how it is, as we cross international and cultural boundaries, and interact and learn new things from others, and put our own spin on what we do.

As Christian Petersen points out, no recipe is written in stone. Living cultures, like the preparation of food, are subject to change, experimentation and adjusting to the times. We are constantly modified by the influences around us.

There is perhaps one small truism that underlies the success of any recipe you choose to follow. The quality of the ingredients measurably affects the taste and goodness of the dish you are preparing. The fresher the ingredients, and the more care taken to grow and produce healthy, nutritious vegetables, grains, fruit, herbs, meat or dairy for your culinary creations, the better they will be. For that reason we recommend using fresh, locally grown, organic ingredients wherever possible.

The other intangible, of course, is the love and caring that goes into the preparation of these delicacies. But we'll leave that up to you.

—Sage Birchwater

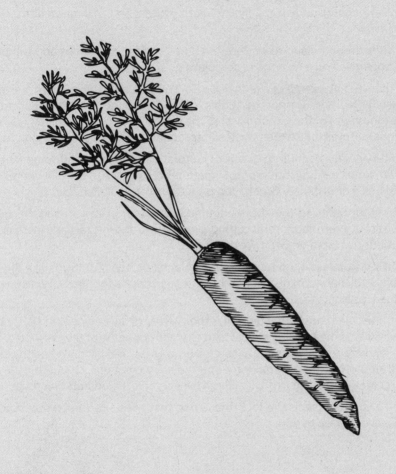

Tastes
of the
Americas

Susan Hance

Susan Hance was born and raised out west at what was called the Salmon River Ranch, which lies within her Dakelh (Southern Carrier) family's traditional lands. Her parents, Patrick and Minnie Sill, raised sixteen children, including two of Patrick's own children.

Try to imagine Patrick and Minnie raising sixteen children in a bush home out west, with no amenities and living almost entirely off the land. Susan was the oldest and naturally her mother's main helper. The family did everything together, including hunting, trapping, fishing and gathering plants for food and medicine. Family survival depended on knowing every plant and animal in the wilderness and how to use them. They relied on moose, deer, caribou, mountain sheep, mountain goat, bear, muskrat, beaver, geese, ducks, grouse, salmon, trout and sturgeon for food. They used the hides of animals and all the edible organs. Nothing went to waste. Susan has a large picture book where she has listed, with photographs, many of the plants and berries they used to rely on for food and medicine. She still remembers how to prepare these plants, where to find them, what time of year to pick them, and how to store them for winter.

Once, when Susan was young, the family was on a horse-packing hunting trip for winter meat. Susan's mother, Minnie, forgot to bring the frying pan and bowls

Dakelh (Southern Carrier)

Moose Tripe

Tripe

Water

2 tbsp (30 mL) salt

Butter

Clean the tripe well. Put it in a large pot and add water and salt. Boil for 2 to 3 hours, then fry with butter in a skillet.

Ready to chow.

My parents, Patrick and Minnie Sill, taught me a lot about traditional foods, and how to preserve them. One morning my mother instructed me to clean the tripe, and off they went to hunt. I tied a heavy string on the tripe and put it in the creek to clean. When my parents returned they noticed right away and said, 'You're taking all the flavour out of the tripe!'

—Susan

Opposite: Susan Hance (left) and Beverley Charleboy bringing in a big salmon.

to prepare meals for all the children. This upset Susan because it was her job to make the bannock for the hungry youngsters and she could not imagine how she would do it. Minnie told her not to worry. Dad was over cutting what looked like sticks for marshmallows. Minnie started building a large bed of stones. After completing the stones, she fished around in the horse packs and pulled out a piece of plastic, which she laid on the stones, tucking the edges under the outer rocks. "There's your bowl, now make the bannock."

Susan went about making the bannock, not knowing how she could cook it with no pan. Minnie came over with the sticks her dad had cut and told Susan to wrap the wet bannock over the sticks and cook it over the fire. Everything was cooked over the fire that night and for the rest of the hunting trip.

Minnie taught Susan how to cook, and there were no recipes and no measuring cups. Susan learned all her skills by watching, asking, helping and doing. The daily lessons were the essence of family life in the wilderness for all the children.

Susan currently works in the First Nations department at Columneetza Senior Secondary. She speaks fluent Carrier and English and is often enlisted as a translator for the courts and medical system. What Susan shared with us here barely scratches the surface of her knowledge. She hopes to someday write a book chronicling her knowledge and experiences.

—Tom Salley

Darlene Doskoch

Don't let Darlene's blond hair and blue eyes fool you. She will very proudly tell you she is Native American—Lenape—and holds her family heritage dear. She and her husband, Lester, are committed Cariboo residents and have raised their two children, Lenette and Dillian, here.

Darlene's fifth-generation great-aunt, Mah Wah Taise (1804–1912), was a healer and a revered woman in the Turtle Clan. Her journey to becoming a legend began when she was about eight years old. While travelling with her mother on horseback, the horse lost its footing while crossing a river. The horse and her mother died, but Mah Wah Taise survived. As she later told the story, "Otter Woman and Tiny Man Woodpecker" saved her. Otter Woman, having saved her from drowning, fed her fish from the river, and Tiny Man Woodpecker brought her nuts and berries, enabling her to survive until her clan members found her.

This was the beginning of a very long life in which Mah Wah Taise became a healer not only of physical injuries, but of emotional wounds as well. After the murder of her only son, the Turtle Clan began to prepare for war against the Osage Tribe. Mah Wah Taise stopped the warriors from waging war and instead invited the Osage leaders to a potlatch. Thus began the talks that led to the cessation of war between the two tribes.

Mush

3 cups (720 mL) water

1 cup (250 mL) yellow cornmeal

Put water in saucepan and bring to a boil. Turn down the heat before you add the cornmeal, but make sure it maintains at least a simmer. Add cornmeal a little at a time and whisk vigorously between additions so you don't get any lumps. Wear a pair of oven mitts so the cornmeal doesn't bubble up and burn you!

If you want to be creative, you can add mushrooms or peppers or anything else you prefer.

As soon as a wooden spoon stands up by itself in the cornmeal, it's ready. Pour into a loaf pan, but not too deep or it will be difficult to cut into slices. A glass cake pan works well. Let sit overnight. Slice into ½-inch (1-cm) or smaller slices. The thinner the slice, the crispier it is. Fry the cornmeal in a light oil of your choice (not olive oil). Be patient; it takes a while to learn to fry the slices just right. Fry until light golden brown on both sides and crispy. Serve with your regular bacon and egg breakfast!

At the age of 108 years old, Mah Wah Taise passed away. She tilted her head back to laugh at something a member of her family had said and took her last breath.

One of Darlene's ancestors, Robert Cushman (1578–1625), was instrumental in helping to organize the *Mayflower* for its maiden voyage to the New World. He was an integral part of the survival of the pilgrims. His mission from London required that all the pilgrims sign an agreement to ship their acquired wares to London in exchange for further support. Despite a pirate attack and a difficult sailing, Robert was able to return to London with the signed agreements, thus ensuring the survival of the Plymouth colonists.

Robert delivered the first "recorded" sermon of the New World, "The Dangers of Self-Love and the Sweetness of True Friendship," which encouraged the pilgrims to take care of their neighbours and focus on the colony's survival instead of their own personal gains. This is a message that is near and dear to Darlene's heart.

Today, Darlene is the Pay It Forward Day founder/coordinator for Canada. Nearly four hundred years later she is delivering the same message Robert Cushman gave to the *Mayflower* colonists.

—Darlene Doskoch with
Marilyn Livingston

George Keener

George Keener is well known around these parts. He is a respected elder and is one of the founders of both the Cariboo Friendship Society and the Xat'sull Heritage Village at Soda Creek. It's clear he's no stranger to hard work. When George was kicked out of the mission school at nine years old, he went to work as a chore boy for a dollar a day at the Cotton Ranch near Riske Creek. At age eleven, he got a job near Alexandria moving railway ties for $2.50 a day. At that job, he wasn't given room and board, so he had to learn to cook for himself. Since then, George has often been called upon to prepare food in a traditional First Nations way for gatherings and workshops. One of his specialties is pit cooking. This method of roasting meat, fish and vegetables in a hole in the ground was used mainly for ceremonies and feasts.

When George talks about food, it turns into a conversation about history, culture, geography and biology. It is amazing how many plants in our own backyards are available for us to eat. Witch's hair, also called deer moss (the dry lichen that hangs from the trees), is not only a good fire starter, but is also rich in vitamins. You can eat it right off the tree or wrap it on a stick and steam it over a fire.

Sunflower roots (balsam root) and tiger lily bulbs can both be cooked and have

Secwepemc (Shuswap) & Tsilhqot'in (Chilcotin)

Birch Basket Rice

4–6 cups (1 L–1.4 L) water

1 cup (250 mL) rice

Traditionally, families would have had watertight birch baskets of varying sizes. You can use a big pot if you don't have a basket. Adjust quantities as you wish but maintain a ratio of 1 cup rice to 4 to 6 cups water (250 mL rice to 1 to 1.4 L water).

Make a fire. Put about a dozen cooking rocks, about 1 to 3 inches (2.5 to 8 cm) in diameter, in the fire. Lava rocks work best because "What comes from fire will be used in fire."

Fill the basket or pot with water and set beside the fire. Wait until the rocks are red hot and then drop them into the basket or pot, 6 or 7 at a time. Add the rice. The water should be at a steady boil. When the water starts to lose its boil (after 20 minutes or so), take those rocks out and replace them with fresh red-hot rocks. Keep replacing rocks until there is only a thin layer of water covering the rice. Then put a lid on the basket or pot and let it steam until the water is gone.

George and his brothers used to call this ant eggs or maggots to gross out their sisters!

Pit Cooking

Start a fire and put in 5 to 10 rocks, about 8 to 10 inches in diameter (or up to 15 to 20 rocks for a 60 lb/27 kg roast). Heat them for 2 to 3 hours until they are red hot.

Prepare food while rocks are heating. Foods to use include meat roast, salmon (skin on, gutted and cleaned, head optional), potatoes, carrots, skinned onions and turnips. Vegetables can be left whole and unpeeled (except for onions).

Dig a pit 2 feet by 3 feet (60 cm by 90 cm), and 3 feet (90 cm) deep.

Line the pit with the red-hot rocks. Lay boughs of willow, chokecherry, birch, alder, poplar or cottonwood on the rocks. Some people use fir. First lay down a 3-inch (8-cm) layer of coarse boughs; next a thinner layer of finer boughs. Follow this with a 3-inch (8-cm) layer of grass or leaves. Place the food on top. Then add 6 to 8 inches (15 to 20 cm) of finer boughs. Place a hide over top, or use canvas.

Traditionally the hollow tube of a rhubarb seed stalk was inserted along the side as a vent and water shaft. You can use a stick. Pour about 1 quart (1 L) of water into the pit. For salmon, potatoes, carrots, onions and turnips, let cook for about 4 hours. A 60-lb (27-kg) roast would take about 12½ hours.

a similar flavour to sweet potato. Prickly-pear cactus was enjoyed as a first green delicacy of spring. The spines can be burned off and the flesh can be eaten peeled or unpeeled. Roasted over the fire, the insides can be squeezed out like a marshmallow.

In the days when a trip to the grocery store was either impossible or a long day's journey, staple foods included vegetables such as wild potatoes and wild onions, salmon and wild meat. Game was plentiful and deer, elk, mountain goats and bighorn sheep were all hunted. Moose were not present in this region until the early 1900s, when they became a regular part of the diet. Another typical food that one might not expect for this area was wild rice. It was a staple even in the days before the Hudson's Bay Company was established, obtained in trade with First Nations peoples from the prairies.

One might think that with a lineage as varied as George's—his roots are Sec-wepemc, Tsilhqot'in, Scottish, Irish and Sioux—it might be difficult for him to know who he is. But George is firmly rooted here in the Cariboo Chilcotin, secure in the knowledge of his land, people and heritage, as passed down to him by his elders.

—Margaret-Anne Enders

Salmon

This recipe calls for salt sage, also known as buffalo sage or ground sage. This is not sage-brush or grocery store sage. You can find salt sage along dry sidehills. It is blue-green and very soft and silky.

CAUTION: Make sure you have properly identified any wild plant before ingesting. If in doubt, substitute!

1 salmon, skin on, gutted and cleaned

Handful of fresh salt sage

6 green onions, peeled and whole

Stuff the salmon with the sage and onions and wrap in tin foil. Cook salmon on a grill over an open fire for about 20 minutes or in a pit for 4 hours.

Secwepemc (Shuswap)

Bannock
(Fry bread)

Makes 12 medium-sized fry breads

3 cups (720 mL) flour (any type)

2 tsp (10 mL) baking powder

Dash of salt

3 tsp (15 mL) sugar or syrup (optional)

2 cups (475 mL) water

Lard or oil (1/16 inch/2 mm deep in frying pan)

Mix dry ingredients together. Add water and mix into a ball. Flour hands and scoop a small ball large enough for one bannock. Pinch into a flat circle about ⅛ inch (4 mm) thick.

Heat lard or oil in frying pan on medium heat. Fry each bannock until brown on both sides. It will rise and be about 1½ inches (4 cm) thick when done.

Enjoy with stews or as a sandwich. Store in a plastic bag or closed container. Will keep 2 to 3 days at room temperature or 5 days in the fridge.

Andrea Thomas

Andrea Thomas is Secwepemc and lives in the Sugarcane community at the east end of Williams Lake. When Andrea speaks, it is clear that she comes from a place of old wisdom and of deep connection to her heritage and people. She's also a great cook. Her bannock is sought-after in her community and she makes delicious Sxusem (hooshum) juice (made from soopollalie or soapberries, also known as buffalo berries). Her Sxusem juice is both bitter and sweet, and very refreshing. As Andrea shares her food, she tells fascinating stories about a time in British

Columbia's past when the nourishment of the body came from the land and not from a package.

Andrea grew up in the Kamloops area, with four grannies as mentors and guides. The grannies on her mom's side taught her about the land and harvesting, while those on her dad's side instilled social and economic values. "You need to go and find your way around and use your voice," they told her.

Long ago people worked a lot, but life was not as fast-paced as today. "You had a lot of time, and you would take the time you needed to get the job done. You also needed to do it with quality, and when harvesting, not disturb the surrounding area."

Respect for the land and the water was key.

In the spring, Andrea and her family lived down by the South Thompson River. Come winter, they headed up into the mountains by Andy Lake. The family lived in cabins by the river and in the mountains, but camped as they travelled by horse and wagon between the two. The kids would walk and harvest what was available as they went along. Their diet was amazingly diverse. The spring began the season of harvesting wild fruits and vegetables as well as plants to be used for medicines. Asparagus, potatoes, carrots, celery, onions and all sorts of berries were plentiful. There were twenty different kinds of

Cedar-planked Salmon

Salmon steak or fillet

Salt and pepper to taste

Soak cedar board for at least 2 hours or overnight. Cedar board can be used directly on hot coals on a fire or on a BBQ grill. Prepare salmon steak or fillet by sprinkling with salt and pepper or use any marinade or rub you prefer.

Place fish on the board, skin side down or flat if using steaks. Place board on BBQ or coals for 5 minutes. Flip fish and cook for another 5 minutes. Serve on a plate of rice with garnish of your choice.

Sxusem (Hooshum) Juice

Soopolallies, also known as soapberries, or Canada buffalo berries, grow throughout the Cariboo Chilcotin, even in town.

⅓ cup (80 mL) soapberries, fresh or frozen,

4 cups (1 L) water

Sugar or honey to taste

Mix all ingredients in a pitcher and stir to squish the berries. Sweeten to taste. Add ice if desired and enjoy.

Soopolallie (Hooshum) Ice Cream

⅓ cup (80 mL) soapberries, fresh or frozen

3 tbsp (45 mL) sugar

1 tbsp (15 mL) water

Put berries in a bowl. Beat with a whisk until they begin to froth. The mixture looks like very little to start, but it will begin to grow. When it starts to expand, add water and sugar and whisk again. Whisk until it is the consistency of whipped cream. Best eaten with a small spoon!

fish, as well as deer, moose, frog, snake, partridge and wild turkey. In the winter, they ate what they had preserved as well as fresh wild game and fish.

Bannock was a staple and was reliable for filling bellies. Back then, they used cornmeal or bulrushes, dried and ground. Flour could also be made by grinding dried meat or dried fruit. Bannock was good travelling food, important as they travelled a lot. Andrea's family was quite self-sufficient, buying only a few treats like wieners and ice cream, and oil for a change from the usual lard. One of her grannies would travel and trade for sugar cakes, kelp and salt from dried salt lakes.

Andrea moved to Williams Lake twenty-eight years ago. Her husband, whom she met doing rodeo during high school, was homesick and wanted to move back to Sugarcane. She now shows her granddaughter, Desta, the ways of the land and how to find her own voice. "She's just a little treasure," Andrea beams.

—Margaret-Anne Enders

Meline Myers

Meline Myers was born in a tent in the Stoney (Yunesit'in) community west of Williams Lake in mid-May. "It must have been cold," Meline muses. Her family was in the process of building a log house, but it was not yet finished, so they spent the spring in a tent. Meline was a couple of months old when they moved into the house. It became the family home and her brother lives in it to this day.

From an early age, Meline had a love for berries, a love that was passed down from her mother, Helena. At age nine or ten, she recalls helping her mother pick berries, all kinds of berries: saskatoons, soapberries, raspberries, blueberries, crowberries and chokecherries. Her siblings would also help. Since there were eighteen kids, even if some weren't around, they would pick a lot of berries. When the picking was done, Helena would dry the berries and Meline's sister Margaret would make pies or pudding. Meline recalls that the soapberries would be cooked and strained and spread out on timbergrass to dry in the sun. Saskatoons and chokecherries would be spread out to dry on denim canvas on the roof.

In the winter, those berries would show up again in treats like saskatoon pudding, berry cake, or Indian ice cream. Meline's family was quite self-sufficient. They mostly ate wild game and vegetables they

Tsilhqot'in

Saskatoon Pudding – Dig Taẑel

2 cups (475 mL) dried berries (saskatoons or chokecherries)

4 cups (1 L) water

½ cup (125 mL) flour (or tapioca flour or pearls)

½ cup (125 mL) water

Sugar to taste

Boil 4 cups (1 L) of water, add berries and simmer for half an hour. Make a paste with the flour and ½ cup (125 mL) of water. Slowly add flour paste to the berry pot. Add sugar bit by bit to taste. Simmer until the berries are cooked and the mixture is thick like pudding, about 10 minutes. Serve pudding warm in a bowl.

Half-dried Meat on a Stick

5 lbs (2.3 kg) moose or deer meat with a bit of fat on it

Salt

To make this delicacy, you first have to half-dry the meat. You can use ribs with fat on them or a flattened-out rump roast. Choose a piece that is about 10 to 12 inches (25 to 30 cm) long by 5 or 6 inches (12 or 15 cm) wide.

Cut it flat, half an inch thick, and put it over a rail of sticks to dry in a smokehouse/shack with light smoke until half-dried, about 2 or 3 days.

Make a fire, not too big. Use dry wood—birch, poplar or pine, but not pitch.

Choose a stick about 3 feet (1 m) long. Willow and young pine are both good. Shave off the bark and sharpen both ends. Push the stick through the bottom of one side of the meat and weave it to the other end. The half-dried meat will be stiff enough so it won't flop over. Push one end of the stick into the ground securely so it doesn't fall into the fire.

grew in their garden—carrots, potatoes, turnips and onions—or foods harvested from the land—wild potatoes and berries. Helena bought sugar, white flour, rice, table syrup, baking powder, yeast, salt, raisins and dried beans, along with pellets and oats for their domestic animals on their occasional trips into town. Before they had a vehicle, they came into Williams Lake by horse and wagon maybe once a summer, often around Stampede time.

Meline treasures the memories of these wagon trips with her mom and dad. They packed up the wagon at other times, travelling to meadows to cut hay for their animals. The older kids went on horseback and the younger ones rode in the wagon. Along the way they snacked on dried meat, tasty to eat and light to carry when travelling. When they were around home, they'd put a bit of butter on top to make it even more delicious. Another favourite for Meline was roasting half-dried meat. They'd take a long strip of half-dried meat from the smokehouse and weave it over a long stick and roast it by the fire. Two such sticks would feed ten or twelve people, enough for whoever was around.

Meline has a deep connection to the sacredness of the land and of the medicines and food that it provides for her people. Her sense of gratitude and respect is vis-

Above: Meline and granddaughter, Nalina.

ible. This attitude shows up in her humility and in her willingness and excitement at the prospect of learning something new. Learning about cranberries is her newest interest. "I've had them once. I've got to learn a bit more."

—Margaret-Anne Enders

If we ever find ourselves in a time of societal collapse, and food from the grocery stores is scarce, I would want someone like Meline to be my mentor and guide. Someone who knows how to put food away and survive the winter without bananas from Chile. Someone who can scan a hillside and see six different edible plants, as George Keener once did out at the Xat'sull Heritage Village. Someone like Andrea Thomas, who has the patience and the skill to dig wild potatoes and onions and forage as she goes. While I hope such a catastrophe doesn't strike, it gives me a certain degree of comfort to know that deep wisdom and connection to the land still exists.

—Margaret-Anne Enders

Slant the other end of the stick towards the fire, flames and coals at a 75° angle. Don't worry; the stick won't burn.

Cook the meat slowly for several hours. Test for doneness by making a slit in the meat with a sharp knife. It should not be red on the inside. Check it every so often.

Once the meat is cooked, consume it right away. It is not like dried meat, which lasts for a long time. If there is some left over, store it in the fridge or cooler and eat it within two or three days.

Mom salts the meat before she dries it, since there could be roundworms on wild meat and salt also helps to dry things faster. But some people can't eat salt, so they dry meat or fish without it.

—Meline

American

Pit BBQ

½ lb (500 g) meat per serving, bone in (less for baron of beef), thawed but firm

1 cord of wood (for large pit)

1 yd (1 m) cheesecloth per chunk of meat

1 yd (1 m) burlap per chunk of meat

1 yd (1 m) chicken wire per chunk of meat

1 steel lid to fit top of pit

Cut the meat into 15- to 20-lb (7- to 9-kg) chunks of uniform size for even cooking. Slice the meat every inch in long slices the length of the chunks but do not cut all the way through.

Sprinkle with salt and pepper to taste. Pour barbecue sauce into the slices in the meat.

Wrap the chunks of meat in cheesecloth, then burlap, then chicken wire.

Dig pit according to amount of meat to be barbecued. A 4x4x4-foot (slightly larger than 1x1x1-m) pit will accommodate 100 to 300 lbs (45 to 135 kg) of meat.

Use dry jackpine, oak or alder. Burn wood down to about 1 foot (30 cm) of charcoal.

Throw prepared chunks of meat into pit and cover with steel lid.

Cover with 8 to 10 inches (20–25 cm) of sand so no air gets in. Watch for smoke

Jeaneen, Hatty and Mandy Thompson

Six months after Jeaneen and Lyman Thompson were married in Aspen, Colorado, they heard a radio program marketing Canada as a great place to settle and populate a country. The idea of fewer people appealed to them because Aspen and much of Colorado were growing quickly and now had too many people for their liking. They came up to the Cariboo thirteen times before they found what they wanted in a ranch out west in the Chilcotin. Then they immigrated.

The couple ran a cow-calf operation of about five hundred head for twelve years while their children, Hatty and Mandy, were growing up. When they immigrated they brought with them a family tradition from Colorado. The family had put on barbecues at several small-town festivals,

particularly the Potato Festival in Carbondale, Colorado. Their Chuck Wagon service typically prepared hundreds of pounds of beef, lamb, pork or buffalo in a traditional pit barbecue, along with all the trimmings on the side. Well, they were a hit in the Cariboo Chilcotin as well. The Chuck Wagon and its wonderful food have graced just about every community event in the Cariboo Chilcotin, from small jackpot rodeos to the Williams Lake Stampede and everything in between.

As it happens, Jeaneen, Hatty and Mandy haven't run the Chuck Wagon for a number of years. They have a small ranch on the way to Alkali that keeps them busy all year, but they are happy to share some of the recipes, tricks and traditions of pit barbecuing that made their Chuck Wagon cookouts such a success.

—Tom Salley

escaping from the pit and cover immediately, otherwise the meat will burn. Cook for 6 to 8 hours depending on the amount of meat. Uncover and eat.

If barbecuing for just family, reduce the size of the chunks and the pit.

Page 35: Hattie and Jeaneen Thompson.

Left: The Thompson family and their Chuck Wagon.

Mexican

Guacamole

4 tomatoes, chopped

1 onion, chopped

½ bunch of cilantro, chopped very fine

Juice of 4 lemons

5 avocados, cut in chunks

3–4 diced jalapeño peppers, depending on heat desired

Mix all ingredients together and add salt to taste.

Chiles Rellenos de Picadillo

6 chilies poblanos*

1–2 tbsp (15–30 mL) cooking oil

Fry chili peppers in oil. While still warm, place them in a plastic bag to sweat. Skin will remove easily. Split chili peppers and clean out seeds.

* The poblano chili is a mild chili pepper originating from the state of Puebla, Mexico.

Maria Guterrez Jackson

Maria grew up in a typical Mexican family in Guadalajara, capital of the Mexican state of Jalisco, with a Roman Catholic background. The Mexican culture is all about family. Maria has two sisters, Maritza and Sabrina, and a brother, Jorge Mario, and a very large extended family of aunts and uncles and many cousins.

Seventeen years ago, Jonathan Jackson was on a holiday from the Cariboo in Maria's hometown, where they met. The two stayed in touch by telephone for two years, there being no internet in those days.

Maria chuckles, "Jonathan was very clever to invite me to Williams Lake in the summer of 1999." During her first day in Williams Lake, Jonathan got a call to go fight fires in the Yukon. He was gone for three weeks. Thank goodness for Sheila and Linda, neighbours of Jonathan and his parents. They took Maria under their wing and treated her as family, using lots of sign language to communicate. Even with this awkward start to her first six months in Canada, Maria said she was instantly in love with the Cariboo.

In 2000, Maria and Jonathan had a large Mexican wedding in her hometown. For the first few years they would spend six months in each country, but eventually settled in Williams Lake as their children, Jose and Jacob, needed to go to school.

When it was time for Maria to spend her first winter in the Cariboo, she says it was amazing. "I still wear double socks, long johns and sweaters."

Maria makes the most of each new challenge. She has learned to downhill ski, she can be seen GT—or extreme—sledding with her children, and she skated for the first time on Williams Lake. How much more Canadian can she be? Maria is also a hockey mom.

Speaking fondly of her large family, Maria misses her culture. She and Jonathan practise Mexican traditions here in Canada, with a family dinner at the table every night, and every September they have a big bonfire to celebrate the Mexican revolution. Perhaps you have heard Maria singing "Viva Mexico"? They also honour the Day of the Dead, and the nativity scene is an important part of Christmas.

Maria says she is very lucky to live in Williams Lake. She loves mother nature, and her family loves to camp. She says she is richer because of the challenges of living in a different culture. "These challenges have enriched my life and I know I am capable of handling bigger things."

—Marilyn Livingston

Picadillo

½ onion, finely chopped

1 tbsp (15 mL) olive oil

1 garlic clove, finely chopped

¾ lb (350 g) ground beef, pork, chicken or tuna

Salt and pepper to taste

1 potato, cooked and cut into small chunks

½ cup (125 mL) chopped tomatoes

1 cup (250 mL) tomato paste

1 carrot, chopped

¼ cup (60 mL) peas

1 cup (250 mL) grated cheese (optional)

Heat the olive oil and sauté onions until soft but not browned. Add garlic, meat, salt and pepper and fry for about 5 minutes. Add potatoes, tomatoes, tomato paste, carrot and peas. Mix and cook until well done, adding a little bit of water. Fill the peppers with the picadillo and sprinkle grated cheese on top.

Red Rice

1 cup (250 mL) uncooked rice

1 tomato, chopped

¼ onion, chopped

2 cups (475 mL) chicken broth

Pinch of salt

1 tbsp (15 mL) olive oil

1 tsp (5 mL) minced onion

1 garlic clove, minced

Mix tomato, chopped onion, chicken broth and salt in a blender and set aside.

Heat olive oil in a medium-sized pot with lid. Add minced onion and the rice, stirring until rice is golden. Add the garlic and the blended mixture. Boil for 2 minutes, turn heat to low, cover pot and cook for 20 minutes or less.

Fried Beans

3 cups (720 mL) cooked beans or 2 cans black beans

2 tbsp (30 mL) vegetable oil

Pinch of dried red peppers

Pinch of salt

½ cup (125 mL) water or juice from the canned beans

Heat oil in pot on medium. Toss in dried peppers. Add beans and salt and fry for 2 minutes. Add water or bean juice. Remove from heat and mash.

When working with hot peppers, it is helpful to wear gloves to protect your hands. Remember not to rub your eyes with your spicy fingers.

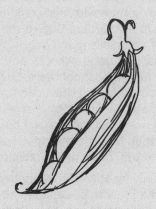

Mary Trott

Mary Trott was born and raised in Bermuda, where her father was a cabinet-maker and her mother a school teacher. Some of Mary's earliest memories are of spending time with her grandmother working in her garden. Due to the influences of colonialism and World War II, Bermuda had good schools and Mary finished her high school there. She went on to study at McGill University in Montreal, where she first got her science degree, then entered medical school. After becoming an MD, she later took specialty training at UBC to become a radiologist.

While studying at McGill, Mary began to realize the breadth of Canada and knew that she wanted to see it all. This desire led her to British Columbia. Once she finished her internship in Vancouver, Mary began to consider her options. At that

Bermuda Black-eyed Peas and Rice

1½ cups (350 mL) rice

3 cups (720 mL) water

2 large sprigs of thyme

½ lb (225 g) bacon

1½ cups (350 mL) chopped onion

¼ cup (60 mL) chopped celery

½ cup (125 mL) diced green pepper

3 tbsp (45 mL) tomato paste

1 beef Oxo cube dissolved in 1 cup (250 mL) boiling water

2 cans black-eyed peas (see sidebar on using dried beans)

Salt and pepper

Dash of hot sauce

Cook the rice in 3 cups of water with the thyme sprigs. Remove thyme after rice is cooked.

Chop and sauté bacon in a large skillet until crisp. Pour off all but 2 tbsp (30 mL) of fat.

To the bacon and remaining fat, add onion, celery and green pepper. Cook until onion becomes transparent.

Add tomato paste and the 1 cup (250 mL) beef stock.

Rinse the canned black-eyed peas and drain. Add beans and the cooked rice to the skillet, along with salt and pepper and a dash of hot sauce. Mix well and simmer for 20 minutes. Turn off heat and let stand for 20 minutes to allow flavours to mix.

Bermuda Codfish Cakes

Any firm-fleshed boneless white fish will do. For example—basa, haddock, snapper or orange roughy—but salt cod tastes the best.

1 lb (500 g) salt cod

1 egg

3 cups (720 mL) cooked, mashed potato (about two medium-sized potatoes)

1 small onion, diced

2 tbsp (30 mL) chopped parsley

½ tsp (2.5 mL) dried thyme

Salt and pepper to taste

Flour

Fine bread crumbs

Canola oil for cooking

Soak the salt cod overnight, in water to cover. Rinse well, put in a pot, add fresh water and bring to a boil. Cook for about 20 minutes or until tender, then drain and flake finely.

Beat the egg in a large bowl. Add the fish and

time, Bermuda was not in need of doctors, and the beauty of British Columbia appealed to her so she took her radiology training and completed her residency in Vancouver. She also had met Bernie Littlejohn by that time, and it so happened that neither of them wanted to live in the city. While shopping around the province for a place to settle, they visited Williams Lake and liked it, and discovered a position for a radiologist.

Mary did a locum at Cariboo Memorial Hospital and liked the staff and people of the area, and it was a fit. Mary and Bernie became permanent residents in October 1975, and shortly after that they decided to start a family. A little later on, young Sonya arrived.

Dried black-eyed peas cook faster if pre-soaked, like all beans, either overnight or using the "quick soak" method:

• Cover the beans with cold water, bring to a boil, and boil for 2 to 5 minutes. Turn off the heat and let them soak for one hour, then drain.

• Cook in three times their original volume of water for at least 45 to 60 minutes or until just tender, giving them the same consistency as canned beans.

—*Mary*

Mary says they found Williams Lake more laid-back than Vancouver. It was easy to make friends here and she connected well with her medical colleagues. When asked why she stayed with so many other options, Mary says it's all about the people, not the place.

Mary shares two traditional Bermudan recipes with us: Black-eyed Peas and Rice, and Bermuda-style Codfish Cakes.

—Tom Salley

mashed potato. Mix well. Add onion, parsley, thyme and salt and pepper to taste.

Form into patties—an ice-cream scoop keeps them uniform—and coat with flour mixed with fine bread crumbs. At this point you can freeze all or part of the recipe.

To cook, fry in ¼ inch (8 mm) of canola oil until golden brown. Serve with tartar sauce.

The codfish cakes go well with baked beans, lettuce or coleslaw and tomato.

Honduran

Pollo en Salsa de Coco
(Chicken in coconut sauce)

1 small chicken, cut into pieces

½ onion, chopped

2 garlic cloves, minced

1 green pepper, diced

1 cup (250 mL) canned coconut milk

2 tbsp (30 mL) soy sauce

1 tbsp (15 mL) sugar

⅓ cup (80 mL) margarine

2 cubes chicken bouillon, crumbled

Salt and pepper to taste

Green platano (plantain)

Sauté onion, garlic and pepper in margarine. Add other ingredients, except chicken and platano, and bring to a simmer. Add chicken. Cover and simmer until chicken is cooked through and sauce is thickened.

Cut the green platano into pieces with the skin on and boil for 15–20 minutes. Peel and serve beside chicken.

Guadalupe Zwez

"Canada's my life now; now it's the only way." It took Guadalupe Zwez quite a while to develop such a fondness for Canada. People come to Canada for different reasons. Many are excited about the prospect of a new life here. Guadalupe, however, came out of love for her husband, who wanted to immigrate to Vancouver from their home country of Honduras. "He was crazy," she laughs. "It's not easy to leave your country." Although Honduras is a poor country, Guadalupe's family was quite well off. In coming to Canada, they were coming to a life starting with almost nothing. In addition, she was leaving behind her parents and nine siblings.

Guadalupe, however, is not the sort of woman to sit and mope. She likes to be busy, shown clearly by the number of careers she has had: microbiologist, secretary, elementary school teacher and nursing aide. While in Vancouver, she raised their daughters, Scarlette and Vannessa, and

worked as a care aide. Once they grew up and set off on their own, you could say that they followed in their mother's footsteps—they both followed their hearts and relocated because of love. Vannessa is in Sweden with her Swedish husband and two children. Scarlette fell in love with the Chilcotin and soon captured the heart of a cowboy in Alexis Creek. Guadalupe moved up to Williams Lake when Scarlette's first child was born. She says she had a lot to learn about country living: "For me, a horse was a horse." Now, three years later, there are two grandchildren, Shale and Torrun, and Guadalupe has learned a lot more about life in the Cariboo—and horses. How could she not, with a cowboy in the family? Although Guadalupe visits her family in Honduras every year, she says, "I cannot move back to Honduras. My home is here."

As it happened, Guadalupe didn't learn to cook traditional Honduran food until she moved to Canada. She enjoys making chicken and rice and big pots of beans and these have been staples for her family over the years. These days, Guadalupe is too busy playing with her grandchildren to spend much time in the kitchen. However, Shale and Torrun love her fresh tortillas, so she always has a pile of them in the fridge for that moment when a yummy snack or a quick lunch is needed.

—Margaret-Anne Enders

Avocado Shrimp Boats

Makes 4 servings as appetizer or 2 as a main course

2 large ripe avocados

Lemon juice

2 medium-sized tomatoes

1 tsp (5 mL) sugar

½ tsp (2.5 mL) salt

Pepper to taste

⅛ tsp (0.5 mL) ground turmeric

1 tsp (5 mL) chopped parsley

2 green onions, minced

1 sprig fresh mint, finely chopped

½ tbsp (7.5 mL) cider vinegar

½ tbsp (7.5 mL) water

Dash cayenne

2 tbsp (30 mL) French salad dressing

1 cup (250 mL) cooked shrimp

Watercress, to garnish

Halve avocados and remove pit. Scoop out pulp and dice it. Rub inside of shells with lemon juice and set aside. Peel and chop tomatoes and add to avocados.

Mix all remaining ingredients except for shrimp and watercress. Pour over tomato and avocado pieces. Mix lightly. Fold in shrimp. Pile mixture into avocado shells. Top with watercress sprigs. Chill before serving.

Tortillas

Makes 10 tortillas

2 cups (475 mL) flour

2 tbsp (30 mL) baking powder

1 tsp (5 mL) salt (or less)

¼ cup (60 mL) margarine

1 cup (250 mL) lukewarm water

Mix flour, baking powder and salt. Add in margarine and mix in by hand. Add water slowly and mix with each addition.

Cover and let rest for 10 minutes in order for baking powder to work.

The secret to a really good tortilla is to roll the dough into 2 long rolls, about 2 inches (5 cm) thick. Cut each roll into 5 or 6 rounds, about 1½ inches (3.75 cm) thick. Lay each round flat. Put your thumb in the centre of the round and press down. Fold the edges up and in to make a little ball. Repeat with the rest of the rounds. Put finished balls in a covered container and let sit for 20 minutes. Roll balls to ¼ inch (8 mm) thick using either a rolling pin or pressing flat with your hands.

Heat a griddle or dry frying pan on medium heat. Flip the tortilla into the pan. Cook it briefly, just until it doesn't stick. Flip the tortilla and cook a little longer on the other side. Flip again. When it puffs up, remove it from the heat.

Notes

Sandy Hart and Sandra McGirr

In a heartwarming twist, this Chilcotin family went to Latin America for one year to share their Chilcotin values of resilience, love of nature and passion for community. Four years later they are still there. Sandy Hart and Sandra McGirr, and their two children, Niall and Tarn, have been living in a village of one thousand inhabitants nestled in the Peruvian Andes in the Sacred Valley of the Incas.

Born and raised in Gatineau near Ottawa, Sandy completed his master's degree at UBC in geomorphology. In 1979 his love of the mountains and backcountry led him and his first wife, Christie, to Tatla Lake. They built a house and office for Sandy's environmental consulting business on their rural property and settled in. Their son, Rob and daughter, Katie both had a wholesome country upbringing and, later, graduated from university.

In 1991, Sandy, now single, met Sandra McGirr, a highly energetic registered nurse who came for a six-week locum at the Tatla Lake medical clinic. They met on Sandra's first day in Tatla and have recently celebrated the twentieth anniversary of their time together. So much for the six-week locum.

Before arriving in Tatla Lake, Sandra had travelled the world. "This is when I gained a picture of the true health situation in other parts of the world," she says, "and

Peruvian

Papa Rellena

Makes 6 servings

2 lbs (1 kg) potatoes

2 raw eggs

1 tbsp (15 mL) cooking oil

1 large onion, diced

1 tbsp (15 mL) minced garlic

1 tbsp (15 mL) ground chili

½ lb (250 g) ground beef or ground chicken

Salt, pepper and cumin seeds to taste

3 hard-boiled eggs, sliced

6 black olives, chopped, pits removed

Flour to coat

Oil to deep fry

Potato Dough

Peel and boil the potatoes. When cooked, mash them together with raw eggs until a smooth mixture is achieved.

Filling

Prepare the filling in a deep pan. Fry the onion, garlic and ground chili until onions are translucent. Add the meat and fry until golden brown. Season with salt, cumin seed and pepper. Add the sliced hard-boiled eggs and olives and set aside.

Assembly

Divide the potato mixture into six individual portions. Using half of the potato mixture for each portion, flatten out into an oval. Place the filling on top of the oval and cover with remaining potato mixture for that portion. With your hands, mould the potato into an oval shape and set aside.

Cover each oval with a sprinkle of flour and deep fry in oil until golden brown.

Serve with lettuce, tomatoes and marinated onion salad—Salsa Criolla (see recipe next page).

knew I wanted to help out in other countries."

Sandra nursed in Tatla Lake and neighbouring communities for sixteen years. During that time she gave birth to their son, Niall, and daughter, Tarn. Then in 2008, when Tarn was ten and Niall was twelve, the family moved to Peru to volunteer for one year. Sandra served as a nurse practitioner in a small health clinic and Sandy established a program installing bio-sand water filters in rural communities. A year later, Sandy and Sandra started a non-profit organization called DESEA ("to wish" in Spanish) Peru to continue the water treatment program and healthcare worker training.

One year has turned into four and Sandra's work has evolved into teaching and training the indigenous women in the remote region to be community health workers, going from home to home in their small villages. Sandra's students are illiterate, so she has designed a complete learning model based on demonstration, artwork and theatre. Empowered by their new-found healthcare capabilities, the women's self-esteem has soared and they are saving lives in their communities.

Sandra was in Williams Lake in November 2012, fundraising for DESEA, and as we spoke her eyes filled with tears as she talked of the giant hearts of the Peruvians. "They need everything and they have nothing, but they offer you what they have," she said.

Fundamental to the people is food. The Incan people come alive when talking about food. "Food is not rushed," Sandra says. "It is about being in the moment while preparing it. It is all about the ingredients and preparation and they are thankful for all of it."

Sandra shares her family's favourite Peruvian recipes.

—Marilyn Livingston

Salsa Criolla

2 red onions, finely sliced

2 hot chilies, finely sliced lengthwise

¼ bunch cilantro, finely chopped

Juice of 2 limes

2 garlic cloves, crushed

Salt and pepper to taste

Mix all ingredients in a bowl and set aside for 30 minutes or more.

Serve on a bed of lettuce with fresh tomatoes and Papa Rellena or beans and rice.

Left: L-R Niall, Sandy Hart, Sandra McGirr and Tarn.

Ceviche de Pescado

(Fish ceviche)

2 lbs (1 kg) solid white fish, cut into 1½-inch (4-cm) cubes

4 garlic cloves, crushed

2 tbsp (30 mL) ground chili

Salt and pepper to taste

Juice of 15 small limes

3 red onions, finely sliced

3 finely chopped fresh chilies

Lettuce for garnish

2 lbs (1 kg) boiled yams, peel on

3 boiled cobs of large-kernel corn

Cut fish into cubes and wash well in fresh water. Drain thoroughly and place fish in a shallow dish.

Add the garlic, ground chili, salt, pepper and lime juice. Cover with a clean towel and leave to marinate for approximately 1 hour.

Boil the yams and peel the skins.

Cook the corn and remove the kernels from the cob.

Ten minutes before serving, add the sliced onions and fresh chopped chilies to the fish.

Serve ceviche on a bed of lettuce with a piece of yam and corn kernels.

Braian and Melissa Barcellos

Braian and Melissa's story began when they met while working on a cruise ship in the Mediterranean. Melissa worked as a ship's art auctioneer and Braian was in sales in the ship's jewellery store. When the possibility of transferring to other ships came up, they made a plan to contract the art auctioneer position as a team so they could stay together. Braian and Melissa travelled the world together for three years and made a bit of money. After three years as partners in life, love and business they decided to return to Brazil, Braian's home, and get married. It was there that Melissa discovered the food of Brazil. She explains that Brazilian food is defined by its freshness, and describes it as exotic and delicious. They both say that processed food or canned goods are rare in Brazil. Food is purchased

Brazilian Stroganoff

1½ lbs (700 g) steak cut into 1-inch (2.5-cm) cubes

¼ tsp (1 mL) seasoning salt

¼ tsp (1 mL) black pepper

¼ tsp (1 mL) garlic powder

¼ cup (60 mL) milk or cream

1 tbsp (15 mL) vegetable oil

1 large onion, diced

2 garlic cloves, minced

½ tsp (2.5 mL) dried parsley

1 carrot, diced

1 cup (250 mL) sliced mushrooms

1 cup (250 mL) tomato sauce or pasta sauce

½ cup (125 mL) cream cheese

½ tsp (2.5 mL) dried oregano

Rub steak cubes with seasoning salt, pepper and garlic powder.

Marinate seasoned steak in milk or cream for half an hour. The milk should make the meat moist but not soaked.

Heat oil in saucepan on medium-high, and sauté onions and garlic until golden brown. Do not burn.

Sprinkle the parsley on the marinated steak and add to the saucepan. Cook until meat is brown on all sides, then add carrots.

Lower heat to medium-low and add mushrooms. Stir and cover for 2 minutes.

Add tomato sauce or pasta sauce and the cream cheese. Stir until it dissolves into an orange-brown cream. Simmer, covered, for 10 to 15 minutes until thickened. This will allow the meat to continue to cook.

Uncover the saucepan, add the oregano and it's ready to serve.

Serve over wild, brown, parboiled or white rice.

on a daily basis at the many open markets in Brazilian towns.

While in Brazil on their extended honeymoon the couple surfed every day on the beautiful beaches and ended each day with their favourite refreshment. They would pick three Brazilian pineapples (smaller than those we eat) and blend them with a few sprigs of mint and ice for the best smoothie this side of Rio de Janeiro.

Braian says his only real draw to Canada was Melissa, who was originally from Prince George. Since arriving in Canada, he has become an avid snowboarder, a qualified insurance broker and a fifty-fifty homemaker. Melissa proudly says they share all the housework. Melissa found a position in Williams Lake in her preferred field of marketing about a year ago, and that precipitated their move to the community.

Braian shares his favourite Brazilian recipe with us, Brazilian Stroganoff.

—Tom Salley

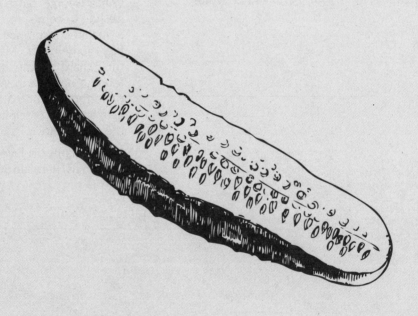

Tastes
of
Europe

Basha Rahn

Basha is a Yiddish name. Basha Rahn's mother named her after her own mother, Basha Freyda, who immigrated to the USA from "old Russia" in the first decade of the 1900s. The family settled in Harrisburg, Pennsylvania, where both Basha's parents were born and raised. Her father, Samuel, was from an orthodox Jewish family, and her mother, Florence, was from what is called a conservative Jewish family.

Basha's family practised the traditions of Judaism. By the age of eighteen, Basha decided to explore a world larger than the traditions and community she was raised in. She attended the University of Wisconsin in Madison, where she earned a degree in anthropology. This piqued her curious nature further so off she went to California and then up to the west coast

Russian

Basha's Mom's Brisket
(Brust)

3 lb (1.5 kg) beef brisket, whole

Salt and pepper

Lawry's seasoned salt

Paprika

Bay leaves

Chopped onion

Water (small amount)

Whole potatoes

Season the brisket with salt, pepper, Lawry's seasoned salt and paprika. In a large pot, sear the brisket on all sides over medium-high heat.

Turn heat to low, cover brisket with bay leaves and chopped onion. Add water to pot—just a small amount in the bottom of pot to keep the meat from burning—and cook, covered, for 2 hours.

An hour before the brisket is done, simmer potatoes in a separate pot, with or without skins.

Remove the meat from the pot and let it cool. Reserve the pan juices. Slice the meat along the grain to make individual servings. Return the meat to the pot with reserved pan juices, add cooked potatoes and reheat.

The Brust was my father's favourite dinner when it came to meat. Meat and dairy are eaten separately in the Code of Law for Kosher, and my dad was a big dairy guy as he had grown up poor and they had more of that than meat. I have never been able to replicate my mother's Brust and I fool myself that her secret was the pot she cooked it in. She had a Waterless Wearever, which created its own juices without ever adding water. Nevertheless, I continue to make what I call pot roasts and they are good, just never like my mom's.

—Basha

of Vancouver Island for a Canadian summer.

She returned to Philadelphia to earn some money and tie up some loose ends, and was back in BC by 1970. To get started she did the mandatory odd jobs, social work contracts and tree-planting stints. By 1980 she had landed a job at the well-

My wife, Ann, and I have been invited to an annual Hanukkah dinner hosted by Basha Rahn and Steve Hunter at their home on Big Lake. It takes place on a Saturday evening which falls during the eight days of this Jewish holiday, during November or December. The appetizers often include smoked salmon, cream cheese, home-made breads, and dips such as hummus and baba ganoush. This is followed by a delicious matzo ball soup. Red cabbage and potato latkes are staples of the main meal, which usually accompany chicken either roasted or braised. For dessert there are chocolate truffles in blue foil, and other fine sweets. Yet what truly makes this meal special, almost ceremonial to my mind, is the traditional meaning of the occasion and the excellence of the company.

—Christian Petersen

known Sooke Harbour House Restaurant on the southern tip of Vancouver Island. She says she was lucky to work under and be instructed by a great chef who worked there at the time. Basha became the dessert cook, among other specialties. In 1982 she was employed by the BC Legislature Dining Room as the pastry chef and worked there for six years.

She met Steve Hunter while living on Vancouver Island, and when Steve was offered a good position with the government in Williams Lake in 1992, they decided to make the move together. When they arrived they found a culture rich with diversity, beautiful landscapes, and a place where it is easy to make good and lasting friendships. It was also a great place for them to apply their professional skills in social and community development.

After being here for a while, Basha realized she was farther away from anything Jewish than she had ever been before. At the same time, people in the Cariboo were very interested in her heritage because they had no knowledge of Jews. She began reconnecting with the traditions she was raised with and got in touch with her mother, Florence, asking for traditional Jewish/Russian recipes. She received them written out in her mother's hand on pieces of paper in different colours and sizes.

Basha shares her mom's recipes for brisket and chicken soup.

—Tom Salley

Basha's Mom's Chicken Soup
(Soup 'n' greens)

1 soup chicken or pullet (not a fryer), cut into quarters or eighths, fat removed

Water to cover

2 celery stalks, chopped, with leaves

2 carrots, sliced lengthwise

Dill weed

Root parsley

Salt and pepper

A few Jamaican allspice

Vermicelli egg noodles, cooked

Put all ingredients, except noodles, in a stockpot and simmer until the chicken is tender (approx. 1½ hours).

Just before chicken soup is done, cook vermicelli noodles and set aside.

Remove the chicken and set aside. Into another pot or large serving bowl, strain the soup through a colander. Sieve the carrots only back into the soup. Shred some of the cooked chicken and add to the soup along with the cooked noodles.

Good for what ails you.

I loved my mother's chicken soup, which was a comfort food for me always. As with all of her cooking, she somehow managed to have it taste the same every time for the hundreds

of times she made it while I lived at home.

On special holidays we had matzo meal dumplings, called knaidlach, in the soup. In my mother's day, they were made from scratch and took a while to make. These days, I get a matzo meal ball mix from the Jewish section of a grocery store and they turn out perfect every time.

—Basha

Chicken soup is deeply engrained in Jewish culture, famous for its mythological healing qualities. It is the basis for the Ashkenazic (Jews from Romania, Germany and Lithuania) Sabbath and holiday meals, with every woman having her own "secret" recipe.

Jerusalem: A Cookbook by Yotam Ottolenghi and Sami Tamimi

Ina Boxeur

Ina Boxeur's parents, George and Mabel Carlson, and their two infant children immigrated to Canada from Sweden in the spring of 1927. They started out in Winnipeg, and when George could not find work they moved to Vancouver, where Ina was born.

Ina first experienced the Cariboo at the age of five, when her family moved to Wells. She has fond memories of that time. After three years they returned to Vancouver. Years later George brought the family to Williams Lake where he started Williams Lake Building Supply, which later became Independent Irly Bird retail lumberyard. Today it is Rona Home Centre.

Ina says that Williams Lake always felt like home. She has lived here for the past sixty years. She and her husband, Emile Boxeur, have six children, eleven grandchildren and five great-grandchildren. All still reside in Williams Lake.

Ina's mother, Mabel, used to tell her children what Christmas was like in Sweden. Christmas Eve was the most important part of the season. The family would bundle up and go to the church in a horse-drawn sleigh for a midnight service. When they got home from church they would each open their present, which would be something practical like a pair of socks. If they were lucky they would also get an orange and some rock candy. Then they

Ina's Mom's Swedish Meatballs

2 lbs (1 kg) ground pork

1½ tsp (7.5 mL) salt

½ tsp (2.5 mL) pepper

2 eggs

1 cup (250 mL) milk

½ cup (125 mL) fine dry bread crumbs

½ tsp (2.5 mL) nutmeg, or to taste

1 small onion, minced

Mix all ingredients thoroughly. Shape into small balls and drop into boiling water. Boil for 5 minutes.

Remove and let cool on a cookie sheet. When they have cooled, they can be used right away or frozen and used when needed. To serve, pan-fry the meatballs or brown in the oven at 350°F (175°C).

"For Christmas we browned them in the oven with cocktail wieners."

Ina's Mom's Pepparkakor

(Spice cookies)

1 cup (250 mL) brown sugar

½ cup (125 mL) molasses

1 cup (250 mL) shortening

1 cup (250 mL) flour (plus extra as needed)

1 tbsp (15 mL) baking soda

1 tbsp (15 mL) ground ginger

1 tbsp (15 mL) cloves

⅓ cup (80 mL) vinegar

Preheat oven to 400°F (205°C).

Mix sugar, molasses and shortening. Add 1 cup (250 mL) flour mixed with baking soda and spices. Add vinegar (it will fizz up) and enough flour to make a stiff dough. Roll thinly, cut into desired shapes, place on greased cookie sheet and bake in a hot oven at 400°F (205°C). Watch very carefully as they only take a few minutes to bake. These will keep a long time stored in a cookie tin. This recipe makes a big batch, so you might want to cut the recipe in half.

would have a smorgasbord supper consisting of pickled herring, cheeses, cold meat, anchovies, meatballs, lutefisk (dried cod) with a white sauce, boiled potatoes, rye bread and hardtack with butter. For dessert they would have rice pudding made by cooking the rice in milk with a couple of cinnamon sticks. They would also feast on cookies and cakes.

Mabel continued the Christmas Eve smorgasbord tradition the rest of her life. After she passed away, Ina carried on the tradition of the family gathering at her home, or at the home of one of her daughters, with as many as thirty family members each year. Christmas Eve 2011 marked the fiftieth year of this celebration in Williams Lake. Ina shares some of her mother's Swedish recipes.

—Ina Boxeur with Marilyn Livingston

Val Biffert

Like many people in the Cariboo, Val is Canadian-born but has roots that wind through the Canadian landscape before reaching back to European soil. Val's great-grandfather was the youngest person, at eighteen years of age, to receive a free parcel of land from the BC government during the first settlement of Norwegians in the Bella Coola Valley. The year was 1894 and he arrived with eighty other Norwegian colonists and their Lutheran

Fårikål

Fårikål is a traditional meat dish from southern Norway. Lamb and cabbage are layered and stewed with peppercorns. It can also be made with pork or venison.

Preparation time: 15 minutes.

Cooking time: 2 hours.

Makes 4 servings

8 oz (225 g) lamb pieces

1 head cabbage, cored and sliced

2 tbsp (30 mL) flour

1½ tbsp (22.5 mL) whole black peppercorns

2 cups or 16 fluid oz (475 ml) water

Salt to taste

Arrange a layer of lamb in the bottom of a casserole or soup pot. Top with a layer of cabbage. Repeat layering as many times as you can. After layering the cabbage and meat, sprinkle the flour and salt on top. Tie the peppercorns into a small piece of cheesecloth or muslin and place in the centre of the casserole. Pour the water over all, and cover with a lid.

Bring to a boil, then simmer over low heat for 2 hours. Remove the package of peppercorns before serving.

Serve with boiled potatoes sprinkled with parsley.

Norwegian Rice Cream

This is a traditional Scandinavian dessert. In certain parts of Norway it is always served at Christmas dinner.

Makes 8 servings

6 cups (1.4 L) milk

1 scant cup (240 mL) regular long-grain rice

3 tbsp (45 mL) sugar

½ tsp (2.5 mL) salt

1 cup (250 mL) heavy cream, whipped

1 14½ oz (400 mL) jar lingonberries

In large heavy saucepan over medium heat, heat milk, rice, sugar and salt until tiny bubbles form around the edge. Reduce heat to low, cover and simmer 45 to 50 minutes or until rice is tender, stirring occasionally. Refrigerate until well chilled.

In small bowl, with mixer at medium speed, beat heavy cream until soft peaks form. Fold into rice mixture and refrigerate to chill well. Serve with lingonberries on top. If lingonberries are not available, use red sauce (recipe next page).

Hint: Add one whole blanched almond to the Rice Cream before serving. The one who discovers the almond will be married the next year. Here in Williams Lake we award an almond pig to the lucky person.

minister, Christian Saugstad. They headed west to British Columbia after their settlement in Minnesota split apart. In order to keep the land, they had to work it for five years and were given five dollars an acre for any improvements. It was tough work and many left, but Val's great-grandfather persevered.

The other side of Val's family tree is Scottish. Her grandfather came to Canada with hopes of new opportunities and good-tasting drinking water. He finally found what he was looking for in Vancouver, but by that time he was running low on money. In order to get back to Scotland to collect his wife and possessions, he had to earn his passage by accompanying a prisoner across the country by train. Fortunately he made it safely and the couple returned to Vancouver to raise their family. Val's mother graduated during the depression and got a teaching post in Bella Coola, where she met and married Val's father.

Val was born and grew up in the Bella Coola Valley. Her mother cooked both British and Norwegian dishes, which Val enjoyed as a young girl. The land and water provided an abundance of food (berries, wild fish and game) for both the Norwegian settlers and the Nuxalk people of the valley. At that time there was no road to the outside and the coastal steamer only came once a week, so self-sufficiency was a must. Despite how difficult that might seem, Val insists they never went without, ever.

Val met Wayne Biffert in Bella Coola while she was working as a telephone operator before the system went to dial. Wayne worked as a lineman for the telephone company, running wires for the new dial system. In 1970 they married and bought nine acres of land near Williams Lake for $882. They still live there with Wayne's fish ponds and Val's gigantic garden. Looking around, Val sighs and smiles, "So, this is home."

Val shares some Norwegian recipes. Fårikål is a traditional recipe that she makes often. She says it's "good the first day, better the second, and damn good the third!" It can also be made with pork or venison. Norwegian Rice Cream is a Scandinavian dessert.

—Margaret-Anne Enders

Red Sauce

1 box frozen strawberries or raspberries

1 cup (250 mL) water

1½ tbsp (22.5 mL) cornstarch

Boil strawberries and water for 5 minutes. Mix cornstarch with a little water and add to the strawberry mixture. Bring to a boil again, stirring constantly until it thickens. Take from heat and cool. Serve on top of the rice cream.

Danish

Lussekatter

These are Danish semi-sweet treble clef-shaped Christmas pastries.

2 packets (4 ½ tsp, 22.4 mL) yeast

2½ cups (600 mL) milk

8 cups (1 kg) flour (approximately)

½–1 tsp (2.5–5 mL) saffron

½ tsp (2.5 mL) salt

1 cup (250 mL) butter

½ cup (125 mL) ground almonds

¾ cup (180 mL) sugar

¾ cup (180 mL) raisins

1 egg

Proof yeast by mixing with lukewarm scalded milk in a large bowl. Add all other ingredients, except raisins and egg, and knead until dough slips off hands. Let rise until doubled in size.

Preheat oven to 400°F (205°C).

Pinch off dough in clumps approximately 3 tbsp (45 mL) in size and roll into long "worms," then form into S shapes. Stick one raisin in the centre of each curl, brush with egg white, and bake for 10 to 12 minutes or until golden. Best served with tea or coffee as a mid-afternoon snack.

Martin Kruus

For Martin's father, Peeter Kruus, and his family, the decision needed to be made now. It was 1944, with the Germans in retreat and the Russian army advancing, ready to reoccupy Estonia as they had after the 1940 Finnish/Russian War. There was a window of just a few days with no occupying army in Estonia.

According to legend, about half the Estonians decided to flee to friendlier countries during this short window because they feared Russia would annex their country. That's when Peeter and his mother and brother got out, hiding in the hold of a fishing boat. Peeter's father had already been conscripted into service by the Nazis.

Peeter spent six years of his youth in a Second World War Swedish refugee camp before immigrating to Canada. Once in Toronto he educated himself and received a Ph.D. in chemistry. While doing his post-doctorate research in Denmark

he met his future wife, Annie, a Danish lab technologist. Annie was also born during the war when Denmark was under Nazi occupation. She grew up to become a very adventurous and confident young woman. When the right man and the right opportunity came along, she was ready to go. They married in Denmark in 1963, and Peeter brought her to Canada to start their family.

As a chemistry professor at Carleton University, Peeter was given a one-year sabbatical every seven years to do research. Peeter and Annie would pack up the kids—Martin, Anders, Linda and Johan—and move to a foreign country for a year while Peeter conducted his research. Martin says that living in foreign countries every seven years had a large influence on his life and his understanding of humanity. He also seemed to inherit some of his parents' wanderlust.

After graduating from high school, Martin

Estonian

Pirukad

This is an Estonian savoury stuffed pastry side dish.

The basic rye (or wheat) flour dough recipe below is followed by two different fillings. Other popular fillings include carrots, eggs, rice, salmon and onions.

Have fun experimenting with these baked dumplings!

Rye dough

6¼–8 cups (800 g–1 kg) rye flour

2 oz (50 g) yeast

2 cups (475 mL) water

1 tsp (5 mL) each salt, sugar

Dissolve yeast in lukewarm water in a large bowl. Stir in sugar and salt. Add flour and mix well.

Cover the bowl and place in a warm spot for 2 hours to let the dough rise.

Preheat oven to 350°F (175°C).

Roll out the dough to ½ to ¾ inches (1.25 to 1.5 cm) thickness. Cut rounds with a large mug, and place 1 tbsp (15 mL) of filling in the centre of each round. Fold in half and pinch the edges to seal. Brush with water or milk. Bake for 15 to 25 minutes.

Meat and Cabbage Filling

1 cup (300 g) sauerkraut

1 tbsp (15 mL) fat or vegetable oil

4 oz (100 g) boiled salted pork or ham, diced

Braise the sauerkraut with fat until soft and add diced meat.

Meat and Mushroom Filling

¾ lb (340 g) cooked meat, minced

5 oz (150 g) mushrooms, scalded and chopped

2–3 tbsp (30–45 mL) butter

2½ oz (75 g) chopped onions

¾ cup (180 mL) meat broth

2 oz (57 g) barley grouts

¾ cup (180 mL) water

Salt to taste

Make a porridge of the barley grouts and water. Mince the cooked meat. Scald the mushrooms in boiling water, chop and add to the minced meat. Sauté onions in butter and add to minced meat and mushrooms, then add the meat broth and grout porridge alternately in small quantities. Mix and season with salt.

Left: Martin and his kids, Ella, Timu and Tobin, enjoying a day in the canoe.

studied at the University of New Brunswick in Fredericton where he received a degree in survey engineering. Not long after graduating, Martin met Catherine, a young occupational therapist. She and Martin hit it off and stuck together while Martin returned to school to earn a degree in education at Nipissing University in North Bay, Ontario. The two young professionals set out on an adventure that included helping the less fortunate in poorer parts of the world. They spent two and a half years in Tanzania, Africa, where Martin taught school and Catherine taught occupational therapy.

When they returned to Canada they decided to move to British Columbia. Williams Lake was the right size of community, offering employment and a great climate, and was surrounded by beautiful wild lands. They made the move and never regretted it. Martin says he knew it was the right place because people were down to earth and sincere. "Where else would you see cars slow down as they passed a neighbourhood mother walking her toddler on the sidewalk?"

Martin and Catherine now have three children of their own and are completely immersed in building a positive community and future for Timu, Ella and Tobin.

Martin shares some Danish and Estonian recipes he learned from his parents.

—Tom Salley

Tine Stace-Smith

Tine was seven years old when her family emigrated from Denmark to Canada. To them, this was the land of opportunity, and they first settled on the British Columbia coast. Tine learned about the exciting gold rush town of Barkerville when she was in grade school, which prompted her to tell her parents about it and ask for a trip to see the town. The family eventually vacationed in the Cariboo and made the requested trip to Barkerville. After that visit, Tine decided she would someday live in the Cariboo. The family loved the Cariboo and subsequent vacations in the area hardened Tine's resolve to someday live there.

Tine met her husband, John, in high school where they became sweethearts. In university John studied forestry while Tine took the education program to become a teacher. It so happened that John's summertime work as a student in the Cariboo turned into an offer of full-time employment in Williams Lake. Tine and John made their move to the Lake Town, where he worked for one of the mills and she secured a position at Scout Island as a teacher naturalist. It wasn't long before Tine was offered a teaching position with School District 27, and she spent most of her teaching career at the 150 Mile School. She loved it, and the school was close to home so her own three children went there too.

Danish

Medister Polser

This recipe requires a meat grinder and the fitting for sliding on the sausage casing.

6½ lbs (3 kg) ground pork

2 medium onions

1½ tsp (7.5 mL) salt

1½ tsp (7.5 mL) pepper

1⅔ cup (400 mL) chicken stock

15 ft (4.5 m) sausage casing

Grind the meat and onions. Use all the fat with the pork or the sausage will be dry. Add the rest of the ingredients and mix well. Fill the casings but not too firmly and twist off about every 6 inches (15 cm). Cook or freeze for later use. Cook in a 50-50 mixture of butter and oil in a frying pan on medium heat and serve hot.

Hint: Use large pork loins when they go on sale and make about 35 lbs (15 kg) of sausage at a time, freezing it into meal-sized portions. Margetts Meat Market in Williams Lake carries sausage casing.

Creamed Kale

Kale is very high in vitamin C and other nutrients.

To prepare the kale, blanch by dipping it in boiling water and then cool in ice water. With your hands, squeeze off as much moisture as you can and then push through a meat grinder. Package in ½-cup (125-mL) portions in small zip-lock bags or containers. Bags flatten better and take less freezer space.

½ cup (125 mL) prepared kale

2 tbsp (30 mL) butter

4 tbsp (60 mL) flour

2 tsp (10 mL) sugar

1 cup (250 mL) milk

1 cup (250 mL) water

Melt butter, add flour and make into roux. Slowly whisk in liquids. Add sugar, boil until thick, then add prepared kale straight from the freezer and stir until everything is hot.

Caramel Potatoes

1 lb (454 g) small, round potatoes

½ cup (125 mL) white sugar

2 tbsp (30 mL) butter

Cook potatoes until just soft. Set aside.

In a large frying pan, melt sugar over medium

As Tine and John approach retirement and consider the possibility of leaving the Cariboo, they have no regrets. Tine says, "Williams Lake has been a great place to raise our family."

—Tom Salley

My mother would always peel the potatoes just after cooking, but my daughter leaves the peels on.

—Tine

heat, watching constantly (it will burn quickly unattended). Don't begin to stir until mostly melted and beginning to brown, then stir until completely melted. Add butter, stirring constantly until the sugar and butter have melted and blended. Add the cooled potatoes, coating them with the caramel until they are hot all the way through—about 15 minutes. Serve immediately with Creamed Kale and Medister Polser... comfort food at its best.

Tine (left), her husband, John, and their daughter, Edilawit.

Belgian

Yogurt

Yogurt starter can be purchased at any health food store.

6 cups (1.4 L) milk

Yogurt starter

Heat milk to 180°F (85°C), then allow to cool to 110°F (45°C).

Remove 1 cup (250 mL) of cooled milk and stir in starter according to package instructions. Add to cooled milk for the first batch. Once you have made the first batch of yogurt, just add a little of the milk/starter mixture to the next batch to start it. Store starter mix in the fridge.

Preheat oven to 170°F (75°C).

Put the cooled milk in the oven and turn off the oven. Ten hours later you have a great batch of yogurt. Store in the fridge.

Granola

10 cups (2.4 L) organic oats

1 cup (250 mL) organic sliced almonds

1 cup (250 mL) sunflower seeds

1 cup (250 mL) pumpkin seeds

1 cup (250 mL) crushed walnuts

1 cup (250 mL) wheat germ

1 cup (250 mL) brown sugar

Carl Johnson

Belgium was the home country of Carl Johnson's mother, Marie Lelieart. She came from the small town of Maldegem. Carl says his mother had genuine style, a marvellous deep laugh and a rich joy of life. When Marie was a child, butter, eggs and cheese were a large part of her diet. Fortunately her papa, Victor, was the local eggs, cheese and butter merchant. He was the first one in Maldegem to have a car. Marie said the car started at one end of town and finished at the other end.

Carl never met his grandfather, though he once visited Victor's best friend, Charles, in Lille, France. Charles was in his early nineties at the time, blind, and he shuffled

when he moved across the room, but he did so with great energy and gusto. When Carl asked Charles about Victor, he says he will never forget his reaction. "Victor! Hu Hu." His booming voice filled the room with joy, enthusiasm and fun!

Late in settling down, Carl got his first regular job when he was forty-two. Two years later he owned a business in Oyama, BC. One day a customer came in and asked him, "If you were to set up any business, what business would it be?" Carl answered, "A dollar store." Realizing that the life expectancy of his business in Oyama was not long, Carl took action and asked a friend, who was a sales rep, where he should build a store. His friend suggested Williams Lake. "This was a place I had never been," Carl says, "but I'd heard of other businesses that had great success in Williams Lake."

He called a local realtor and asked for a retail space close to a drugstore in the downtown area. A funny thing happened the next day. Carl ran into two former employees from his business in Oyama, David and Joanne Rose, and offered both of them jobs on the spot. David helped renovate his new store and Joanne helped run it.

Eggs, milk and cheese always remind Carl of breakfast, so he decided to share his favourite breakfast recipes.

—Carl Johnson with Tom Salley

1 tsp (5 mL) cinnamon

1 cup (250 mL) honey

1 cup (250 mL) cooking oil

Preheat oven to 325°F (160°C).

Combine all dry ingredients in a roasting pan and stir in all wet ingredients. Put filled roasting pan in the oven. Stir every 2 to 3 minutes for the next 40 minutes and you'll have really good homemade granola.

Crepes

This recipe turns out well if the batter is allowed to rest overnight.

Makes about 7 crepes

4 eggs

1 cup (250 mL) milk

1 cup (250 mL) flour

1 tbsp (15 mL) melted butter

Dash of salt

Combine all ingredients in a mixing bowl and whisk vigorously. Rest the batter in the fridge overnight.

Oil a good crepe pan and heat to medium-high.

Use about ½ cup (125 mL) per crepe. Let the crepe bubble and then flip it in the air and cook it on the other side for about 15 seconds.

Serve with maple syrup.

German

Mock Cream Cheese

Healthy, delicious and a great substitute for quark.

Use one carton of the best-quality Bulgarian-style yogurt. Empty contents of yogurt carton into a double layer of cheesecloth, bundle it and hang it on a hook over a bowl. When it stops dripping, it's ready.

You can drink the whey and use the luscious cheese instead of quark or cream cheese.

It's so much lower in fat and calories, and some of my friends use it instead of butter. It is fabulous as an appetizer with pepper jelly.

—*Krista*

Kassler with Mustard Sauce

This recipe calls for smoked pork loin with rib bones, available at any German butcher. Count on one rib piece per serving. If smoked pork loin is not available, substitute smoked picnic shoulder, which is very juicy and just as good.

Smoked pork loin, 1 rib piece per serving

1 large package coleslaw mix

2 ribs celery, sliced very thin

1 large carrot, roughly shredded

Krista Liebe

Krista Liebe never intended to immigrate to Canada. After finishing her academic baccalaureate and before starting her final studies, she wanted to fulfill a childhood dream and take the "big ship" overseas. That was very unusual at the time. She was young, single and had great opportunities ahead. She spoke German, English and French fluently.

Krista didn't know a soul in Canada, and the boat trip was a big disappointment. The ship was loaded with immigrants and most of them were full of melancholy about what the future held for them. On advice from her counsellor at the Canadian Embassy in Bonn, Krista arrived in Calgary in the middle of April, and a few days later experienced her first real snowstorm. She quickly met people and made some friends—friendships that have lasted to this day.

Her first authentic Canadian meal was unforgettable. To save money Krista had been living on bread, jam and milk. When a middle-aged couple heard of this, they invited her for a supper of mashed potatoes, ham and creamed corn. The mashed potatoes were fine, the ham was a bit dry and very salty, but she gagged on the creamed corn. After a few tries at this sweet, gooey substance, she had to admit that she just could not get it down. Her hosts, Bob and Earla, expected that reaction, and laughed heartily at her desperate attempt to be polite.

After supper, Bob got his toothpick and went to work cleaning his teeth. Krista did not know where to look. Then Earla did the same. They kept on poking while they were talking to her, which surprised Krista because she had thought they were such a nice, educated, upper-middle-class couple.

Bob was one of the managers of the Royal Bank in Calgary and arranged for Krista to get her first job in Canada. The day after their supper he took her out to try root beer. Krista squirmed and swallowed.

1 large chopped onion

1 can of sauerkraut

10 juniper berries

Mix all ingredients, except the meat, in a roasting pan. Place the Kassler or picnic shoulder on top, cover the pan and put in the oven. Cook at 375°F (190°C) for 1½ hours.

Mashed Potatoes

1–2 potatoes per serving

Small container of cottage cheese

2–3 chopped green onions

Boil potatoes in water until soft. Drain the potatoes, reserving the water. Mash potatoes and mix in the cottage cheese and onions. Place the mixture in a buttered glass dish and bake uncovered with the roast in the oven for the last 20 minutes.

Mustard Sauce

2–3 tbsp (20–45 mL) olive oil

2–3 tbsp (20–45 mL) flour

1 cup (250 mL) or more of reserved potato water

Salt

Prepared mustard

Heat olive oil in saucepan and mix in flour. Very lightly brown the mixture. Pour in the saved potato water and more water (if required), stirring vigorously. When cooked through, add salt and prepared mustard to taste. Be generous with the mustard and experiment with different types. The sauce should be quite tangy.

Serve with Kassler and mashed potatoes.

Rote Grütze

As a Northern German, Krista uses her extensive fruit garden to serve a "Rote Grütze" for dessert.

1 cup (250 mL) tapioca

2 cups (475 mL) water

1 cup (250 mL) each of available berries—black and red currants, sour cherries, gooseberries, raspberries, blackberries and strawberries

½ cup (125 mL) sugar

Fresh lemon juice

Boil the tapioca in about two cups of water. When tapioca is translucent, add the fruit.

Bring to a boil and add the sugar and some fresh lemon juice. Turn heat off and let cool completely. This can be prepared in the morning and kept in the refrigerator.

Just before serving, prepare your favourite vanilla custard and pour over the cold fruit mixture.

Guten Appetit!

Later she sent cans of root beer and creamed corn to her family and friends back in Germany. How else could they believe this stuff?

This was the beginning of a long relationship with a beautiful country. Krista found her freedom by accepting the challenges given her and using them for the best outcome possible. On her own little farm she raised and milked cows by hand; she started and operated a highly successful translation agency; she produced a live German-language radio program in Edmonton for over fourteen years, and took on many other endeavours.

With her husband, Tihol Tiholov, a school psychologist, she moved to Williams Lake and completely fell in love with the truly "Western" lifestyle of the Cariboo Chilcotin. As she always needs a bit more of a challenge, she started a German-language newspaper, *Die Kleine Zeitung mit Herz*, which is now in its ninth year and going strong. Krista and Tihol also started the Williams Lake Film Club, which raises money to support students with learning disabilities.

Krista's cooking is very experimental and is one of her many passions. She has developed a fusion of diverse styles.

—Krista Liebe with Tom Salley

Traudl Marten

Traudl visited Canada and the Cariboo twice during the 1980s while vacationing from Bavaria in Germany. She had friends in British Columbia, especially around Puntzi Lake, and it was through these friends that she was told about a local German man who eventually became her husband. Joe Marten had already immigrated to Canada from Germany and was living near Williams Lake. Traudl and Joe got to know each other through correspondence while Traudl was back in Germany, and they married in Germany in 1991. Traudl promptly completed her immigration so she could return to the Cariboo, and she arrived in 1992.

Knoblauch Suppe

(Garlic soup)

6 cups (1.4 L) beef broth

6–8 garlic cloves, chopped

1 tbsp (15 mL) marjoram

1 tsp (5 mL) caraway seeds

2–3 tbsp (30–45 mL) soy sauce or to taste

Dash of cayenne pepper

Grated Gruyere cheese

1 baguette, sliced in pieces 1 inch (2.5 cm) thick

Heat broth and chopped garlic. Add marjoram and caraway seeds and let simmer for 20 to 30 minutes.

Add soy sauce and cayenne pepper.

Slice baguette and arrange slices on a cookie sheet. Top the slices with grated cheese.

Broil until cheese is melted and golden brown.

To serve, put bread in soup bowls and top up with the soup.

Rindsrouladen

(Beef roulades)

Four 4-oz (120-g) slices of beef roulades (or sirloin sliced thinly)

4 tbsp (60 mL) mustard

8 slices bacon

4 pickles, thinly sliced

2 large onions, thinly sliced

Salt and freshly ground pepper

1 tbsp (15 mL) paprika

2 tbsp (30 mL) oil

1½ cups (350 mL) beef broth

¼ cup (60 mL) red wine

2 tbsp (30 mL) flour

Pound the meat until it is ⅛ inch (4 mm) thin.

Spread mustard on the roulades. Place bacon first, then pickles, then onions on top. Roll the roulades up from the small side and tie with kitchen string to make parcels. Season with salt, pepper and paprika.

Heat oil in a skillet, add roulades and cook, turning frequently, until browned all over. Add the beef broth and any pickles or onions that were left over, chopping them before adding. Cover and simmer over low heat for 50 to 60 minutes.

Put wine and flour in a mason jar with a lid and shake well until no lumps remain.

Traudl's life in the German Alps instilled a love of nature, and when she discovered the natural beauty of the Cariboo it was a match for her. She loved the Cariboo for its freedom, abundant wildlife, and the opportunities it presented for a new life. She finally had time to garden, make wine, sew, knit and cook. She took an ESL (English as a Second Language) course to assist her in the transition.

She and Joe built a good life together, but unfortunately he passed away unexpectedly in 1999. Despite losing her husband, Traudl remained in the Cariboo.

When asked why she stayed, she says she has many friends, a beautiful home and a love for nature. "Where else could you have a momma bear with four cubs come and visit your home regularly while you watch them from the living room window?" Those are the experiences she brags about to her friends who visit from afar. Some people would not believe that a bear could have four cubs, so Traudl has pictures to prove it. Lately, she has been excited about seeing badgers around her place.

Traudl shares three German recipes with us: Knoblauch Suppe (garlic soup); Rindsrouladen (beef roulades), and Schokoladen Kuchen (chocolate cake, gluten free).

—Tom Salley

Remove roulades from the skillet and set aside. Bring pan juices to a boil and add flour/wine mixture. Let cook for a few minutes, stirring constantly. Season with salt and pepper to taste. Return the roulades to the skillet and heat through.

To serve, remove strings from the roulades and pour sauce over the meat. Serve with potatoes or pasta.

Schokoladen Kuchen

(Chocolate cake, gluten free)

7 oz (200 g) dark chocolate

4 oz or ½ cup (100 g) sugar

4 oz or ½ cup (100 g) butter

4 eggs

1 tbsp (15 mL) cocoa powder

7 oz (200 g) ground almonds

Preheat oven to 350°F (175°C).

Melt chocolate in a double boiler and let it cool slightly.

Cream the butter and sugar and add the eggs one at a time, beating with each addition. Beat in the cocoa and chocolate. Fold in the almonds and pour into a 9-inch (23-cm) round cake pan. Bake for 40 to 45 minutes.

Serve with fruit and whipped cream.

Polish

Salatka Warzywna
(Potato veggie salad)

5 hard-boiled eggs

5 dill pickles

1 leek (white part), chopped fine

1 cup (250 mL) peas, fresh or frozen

5 small carrots

2 parsley roots

½ small celery root

3 large potatoes

2 tbsp (30 mL) mayonnaise

1 tsp–1 tbsp (5 mL–15 mL) yellow mustard (optional)

1 tsp (5 mL) sugar

Salt and pepper to taste

Boil the peas, carrots, parsley roots, celery root and potatoes until soft.

Dice leeks and pickles.

Cool the vegetables and peel and dice them as small as you wish.

Mix the hard-boiled eggs, diced pickles and leeks with the cooked, diced vegetables. Add mayonnaise, mustard and sugar and blend everything together. Add salt and pepper to taste.

Decorate salad with pieces of boiled vegetables, boiled eggs or fresh parsley.

Liliana Dragowska

Liliana's father fled Poland for Canada after the Iron Curtain went up. A couple of years later, Liliana, aged three, and her mother and sister immigrated to Canada to reunite with Liliana's father in Vancouver. One of the services that helped the family immensely was the Polish Catholic Church. It connected them with other Polish families and created a support network for them within the parish. Liliana's family were outdoors enthusiasts in Poland, and when they arrived here the parish priest assisted them in finding the outdoors treasures of BC.

As soon as she was old enough, Liliana started attending public school. At the same time, she attended Saturday classes at the church. The classes were designed to help them with the transition to Canada and keep them up to date with what was happening in Poland.

From these beginnings, Liliana went on to earn a degree in civil planning from the University of Northern British Columbia. This led to employment as a civil planner for both the Cariboo Regional District and the City of Williams Lake. She says that she has found her spot in the Cariboo. The culture is still young, growing and changing. She sees the opportunities for making change. Enjoying nature and relishing our freedoms are the elixirs that keep her here.

Liliana still holds close to her heart the part of Poland her mother brought with her—namely, the food. From her mother and grandmother, Liliana learned recipes, techniques and the traditions that still connect her to Poland, the church and family. Three recipes that she shares with us are Salatka Warzywna, a cooked vegetable salad served at Easter, Christmas and birthdays; Makowiec, poppyseed rolls, a sweet bread her grandfather used to eat every day, which is served like cake with tea; and Nalesniki, potato crepes with onion and cheese (Liliana's favourite comfort food.)

—Tom Salley

Makowiec
(Pronounced mah-KOH-vyets)

Dough

1 package active dry yeast or 2 tbsp (30 mL) live yeast

2 cups (475 mL) warm milk (divided)

8 cups (1.9 L) all-purpose flour

¾ cup (180 mL) sugar

1 tsp (5 mL) salt

5 eggs

½ cup (125 mL) butter, melted

In a small heatproof bowl, dissolve yeast in ½ cup (125 mL) of the warm milk.

In the bowl of a stand mixer or a large bowl, combine flour, sugar, salt and eggs. Add remaining 1½ cups (350 mL) warm milk, butter and yeast mixture. With the paddle attachment, or by hand, beat until smooth. Dough will be sticky at this point.

Scrape dough into a clean, greased bowl. Sprinkle the top with a little flour and cover. Let stand in a warm place for 1 hour or until double in size.

Punch dough down and turn it out onto a floured surface. Divide dough in half and shape each half into a rectangle.

Poppyseed filling

1 lb (500 g) ground poppyseeds

1 cup (250 mL) hot milk

1 cup (250 mL) sugar

¾ cup (180 mL) softened butter

1 lemon rind, grated

¾ cup (180 mL) raisins

Soak poppyseeds in milk and put the seeds through a meat grinder or food processor, then combine all filling ingredients. Beat well and set aside.

Spread half of the filling on each rectangle of dough and roll up like a jelly roll. Turn ends under to keep filling inside.

Place on a parchment-lined or greased pan, cover and let rise again until double in size.

Heat oven to 350°F (175°C). Brush tops of rolls with additional melted butter or egg white. Bake 45 to 60 minutes or until rolls are golden brown.

Remove from oven and cool. Dust rolls with confectioner's sugar, if desired.

Liliana and her sister dressed up for a celebration at the Polish Community Hall in Vancouver.

A piece of bread in one's pocket is better than a feather in one's hat.

Nalesniki
Polish Crepes

Depending on the number of servings required, recipe may have to be doubled or tripled.

Crepes

3 eggs

1½ cups (350 mL) milk

1 cup (250 mL) flour

Salt to taste

2 tbsp (30 mL) olive oil

Filling

1 cup (250 mL) chopped onions

2 cups (475 mL) mashed potatoes

1 tbsp (15 mL) butter

3 tbsp (45 mL) milk

1½ cups (350 mL) small curd cottage cheese, drained in a sieve

Salt and pepper to taste

Mix all ingredients for the crepes and allow to sit for ½ to 1 hour.

Place about ¼ cup (60 mL) of runny batter on a crepe skillet or in frying pan. Allow to cook on one side for about a minute and flip. Do not overcook the crepes.

Oh, I love this dish with some good tomato soup.

—Liliana

Stack the crepes and set aside.

Prepare the filling by frying onions with a little butter or oil until golden brown and place in a large bowl.

Boil and mash potatoes with butter and milk. Add potatoes to the onions in the bowl, and add cottage cheese. Salt and pepper to taste.

Place a few tablespoons of filling in each crepe. Fold the sides into the middle and then roll up the ends so that you have a spring roll-type look but a little fatter.

Repeat this for all the crepes and stack on a plate or in a casserole container for storage.

Before serving, heat a frying pan on medium heat with some butter and fry the rolled-up crepes for 2 to 3 minutes per side, heating up the filling and adding a little crunch to the crepe.

Serve warm with sour cream, sauerkraut or on their own.

Ollie Martens

Ollie's parents emigrated from the Ukraine and landed in Canada in the early 1900s. She laughs as she recalls watching her mother cook, but she never really learned to cook Ukrainian until after she was married.

Ollie met her husband, Richard, at a dance in Winnipeg. He was in the Canadian Forces and she was a nurse. One year later they were married and on their way to British Columbia. Richard was from the Burns Lake area and thought BC would be the

Cabbage Rolls

4 heads Savoy or other loose cabbage

Water

8 cups (2 L) rice, cooked until tender

5 lbs (2.3 kg) lean ground beef

2 large onions, diced

Handful of dill weed, finely chopped

Salt and pepper

Butter or margarine

4 tbsp (60 mL) powdered chicken stock

3 to 4 cans tomato soup or equivalent tomato juice

Remove cores from cabbage by cutting around core with a sharp knife. Put enough water in a deep pot to cover one or two whole cored cabbages. Heat water, then put cabbage into the hot water to soften. Do not overcook. Take the cabbage out of the pot (reserve the water) and remove the outer shaggy leaves. Then separate the inner leaves without tearing them. Cut the hard rib out of the leaf to make it easier to roll.

Cook rice and then add raw ground beef. The hot rice will cook the beef.

Add onion and a liberal amount of butter or margarine to the rice/beef mixture. Add salt, pepper and dill weed and mix well.

Roll the rice mixture in the softened cabbage leaves, tuck in the ends and lay them in a roasting pan. Mix the powdered chicken stock with the reserved cabbage water and pour it over the cabbage rolls. Then pour the tomato soup over the cabbage rolls. Cover the rolls with the shaggy outer leaves so they don't dry out during cooking.

Cook in 325°F (160°C) oven for about 2½ hours.

Borscht

Soup base, using chicken or turkey carcass and gravy or pork riblets

6 lbs (3 kg) beets, with stems and leaves, diced or shredded

Vinegar

1 small head of cabbage

A few stalks of celery

1–2 onions

5–10 carrots

4 cups (1 L) canned tomatoes

1 package of fresh dill, finely diced

Sour or whipping cream

In a large pot make the soup base.

Dice or shred the beets and optional stems and leaves and add vinegar to retain the colour of the beets.

In a saucepan, sauté the cabbage, celery and onions.

Richard Martens

place to find employment to support their growing family. Over the years they lived and worked in Decker Lake, Houston and Granisle before moving to the Cariboo.

They arrived in Williams Lake on November 7, 1970, and Ollie says she'll never forget that date because with four young children and a nervous cat it seemed like the longest trip of her life. They had only a couple of days to get settled before Richard had to start his new job at Gibraltar Mines. Once the children were old enough, Ollie eventually went back to work nursing at Cariboo Memorial Hospital.

Ollie started cooking Ukrainian food after she and Richard were married. She credits Richard for being very patient while she learned to cook. She began collecting Ukrainian recipes and cookbooks, and could still envision how her mother made the dough as she prepared the recipes from the cookbooks. "I could still remember Mom's tricks for making the dishes turn out right."

Ollie has perfected her recipes by preparing food for Meals in the Park, the Williams Lake International Food Festival, and many catering contracts. She says the beautiful thing about Ukrainian food is how easily it can be preserved. "You can make a lot of cabbage rolls for a lot of people and just freeze them."

Preparing Ukrainian food is something Ollie and Richard like to do together. They have been married and cooking together for forty-seven years. For this cookbook, Ollie shares her traditional Ukrainian recipes for cabbage rolls, borscht and pirogi.

—Tom Salley

Add beets, celery, cabbage and onion to soup base. Add carrots and any other vegetables desired.

Add the canned tomatoes and dill, and simmer for about 2 hours. Add salt and pepper to taste.

Serve soup in bowls, garnished with sour or whipping cream.

Hint: Portions of vegetables and beets will vary with taste. Add what you like. For variety, use white beans instead of cabbage.

Pirogi

5 lbs (2.3 kg) boiled potatoes (4 cups/1 L of potato water reserved)

1–2 medium to large onions, finely chopped and sautéed

6 cups (1.4 L) cheddar cheese, grated

Bacon bits (optional)

1 tbsp (15 mL) salt

Butter and margarine

6 cups (1.4 L) (or more) flour

6 eggs, beaten

1 tbsp (15 mL) vinegar

1 cup (250 mL) oil

Dough

Mix the flour, eggs, vinegar and oil. Add the reserved potato water in small amounts to make a soft dough and roll it out thinly. Use a pizza cutter to make squares or a glass to make rounds.

Filling

If using bacon bits, cook the bacon on a cookie sheet, then use food processor to crumble it.

Mash the potatoes and add the sautéed onions, grated cheese and bacon bits, if using. Add enough cheese to turn the mixture orange and give a strong cheese flavour. Add salt and pepper to taste. Add generous amounts of butter to mix.

Assembly

Add the filling, pinch edges of dough together and boil in batches for 3 minutes. Do not rapid boil. Remove the pirogi with a slotted spoon and immerse in melted margarine. Place in a sealed container. Once they cool, either freeze them or pan fry them and enjoy.

Hint: Other ingredients for the filling include cottage cheese or sauerkraut. If using sauerkraut, sauté it slowly in a small amount of butter for 1 to 2 hours to soften the cabbage fibres. Use mashed potato/onion mix to hold it all together.

> My German grandmother, Bertha Enders, often made perogies (pirogi). We called them perhay and they were the best I've ever had. She put mashed potatoes in the dough, a variation that I have yet to come across elsewhere. My dad and I continue her legacy and often make them at Christmastime.
>
> —Margaret-Anne Enders

Gloria Atamanenko

Peter Chomiak from the western Ukraine told his sweetheart, Nellie, "I will move to Canada, find work, buy a farm and build you a house for our family. If you come and do not like it, I have the funds to get you back home." Peter arrived in 1926, worked hard and kept his promise. Nellie came four years later, liked it and stayed. One of the great results of that decision was Gloria Chomiak.

Gloria was born near Fort Vermilion in northern Alberta and lived there until she was fifteen. Then she moved to Delaware in the US and stayed with family to complete her schooling. She worked as a social worker for a year before returning home to Alberta. The first summer back she met a young land inspector by the name of George Atamanenko. George's family was from the eastern Ukraine, and Gloria's

Christmas Tree Bread

This bread is a traditional Ukrainian Christmas morning treat. The Christmas tree shape is Gloria's Canadian adaptation.

2 cups (475 mL) lukewarm water

1½ tbsp (22.5 mL) yeast dissolved in ½ cup (125 mL) warm water with 1 tsp (5 mL) sugar

¾ cup (180 mL) butter, melted

2 whole eggs (save a little for egg wash)

3 egg yolks

Grated rind of ½ lemon

3 cardamom seeds, peeled and crushed

½ cup (125 mL) sugar

1 tsp (5 mL) salt

½ cup (125 mL) flaked almonds

Enough white flour to make a soft but manageable dough

Mix all ingredients thoroughly in a bowl and knead well. Cover with a clean cloth and allow to rise for one hour. Punch down and allow to rise again. Punch down and allow to rest for 10 minutes.

Divide the dough into 2 portions and shape each into a triangle. Point the triangle away from you and remove two sections of each triangle, creating 3 legs that rise up to the point (head) of the triangle. Twist each leg several times. Braid the three legs together and slash the edges. These edges will become the branches of the Christmas tree bread.

Place on lightly greased cookie sheet. Brush with egg beaten with a little milk. Allow dough to double in bulk.

Preheat oven to 350°F (175°C).

Bake for 25 to 30 minutes, or until top centre feels firm to the touch and the bottom sounds hollow when tapped.

Cool. Ice with white icing (cream cheese icing flavoured with almond extract works well) and decorate with glace cherry halves and sliced almonds.

from the west. Eventually they both had the opportunity to transfer to BC, and it was long-distance kisses for a while when George found work in Williams Lake and Gloria got a job in Prince George.

Eventually, Gloria was able to transfer to Williams Lake and they married in 1957. From there they moved to Vancouver for specialized education in their respective fields. George studied community planning at UBC and Gloria honed her social work skills by acquiring a degree in counselling psychology. After living in Victoria for twenty-seven years, the Atamanenkos retired to the Cariboo in the 1990s and bought a small ranch in the 150 Mile House area. They remain active in a wide range of interests from politics, ranching, heritage and land use planning to social justice, First Nations and environmental concerns.

Gloria also thrives in the kitchen and shares some of her delectable Ukrainian recipes.

—Tom Salley

Opposite: Gloria and George Atamanenko.

Notes

Medivniky

(Ukrainian honey cookies)

Honey mixture

1 cup (250 mL) honey

¾ cup (180 mL) sugar

½ cup (125 mL) butter

½ tsp (2.5 mL) ground cloves

1 tsp (5 mL) allspice

2 tsp (10 mL) cinnamon

Cookie dough

2 tsp (10 mL) vanilla

6 eggs, separated

2 tsp (10 mL) baking soda

4 cups (950 mL) white flour (or more to make a soft dough)

Glaze

Icing sugar

Vanilla

Cream

(Or icing sugar mixed with brandy or lemon juice)

Mix together the ingredients for the honey mixture on low heat until sugar is dissolved. Remove from heat and transfer to a large bowl. Allow to cool until lukewarm.

For the dough, beat egg whites and vanilla until stiff, and set aside.

Beat egg yolks and stir into the cooled honey mixture. Stir in baking soda. Add flour and blend well. Fold in beaten egg whites thoroughly and add a little more flour if dough feels too wet.

Butter a large platter or pizza pan and turn dough out onto it. Cover with waxed paper and allow to ripen in the refrigerator for 2 to 3 days. The dough will become stiffer and more manageable.

Preheat oven to 325°F (160°C).

Roll out cookie dough to ¼ inch (8 mm) thick and cut with large cookie cutter. Bake until pale golden. (They scorch easily, so watch them carefully.)

Prepare glaze by mixing icing sugar with liquid of choice. It should be the consistency of heavy cream.

Dip the top of each hot cookie into glaze and cool on cooling racks. Store in airtight containers with waxed paper between layers so they don't stick together.

Amidst the richness and depth of the diversity that enlivens the Cariboo Chilcotin lies the basic truth that beneath the differences, we are all simply human, sharing in the common quests of finding meaning, love, and belonging.

—Margaret-Anne Enders

Linda Gorda

Linda Gorda and her husband, Wayne, moved to Williams Lake from Roblin, Manitoba. Linda's father was from Romania, and her mother's parents emigrated from Romania before her mother was born in Canada. Linda and Wayne, with their first child in tow, moved to Williams Lake because Wayne found work there.

Linda found Williams Lake a bit wild when they first arrived. She remembers the bars being packed and few family-oriented activities in town. The young family found themselves exploring the natural wonders of the area, visiting historic sites like Barkerville and taking advantage of the wonderful hunting opportunities.

Despite the growing pains of a once wild and woolly cow town transitioning into a modern community, Linda found that she liked living in Williams Lake. It wasn't just the natural beauty of the area that held her, or the employment options; it was the friendliness of the community and its people that convinced her this was the place for her.

Linda's mother taught her how to cook. She cooks from scratch and by memory and doesn't measure ingredients. This is the first time some of the recipes have been written down and shared. To do this, Linda had to prepare her recipes and measure how much of each ingredient she used.

Paska

(Easter bread)

¼ cup (60 mL) very warm water

2 tbsp (30 mL) sugar

3 tbsp (45 mL) yeast

3 cups (720 mL) water

½ cup (125 mL) sugar

1 tbsp (15 mL) salt

6 eggs, beaten

½ cup (125 mL) oil

6–8 cups (1.4–1.9 L) flour

Mix ¼ cup (60 mL) warm water with 2 tbsp (30 mL) sugar and yeast. Set aside.

In a large bowl, mix 3 cups (720 mL) water, ½ cup (125 mL) sugar, salt, eggs and oil. Mix well and add the yeast mixture. Add flour one cup at a time until a soft dough forms. Knead well and let rise until double in size.

Grease two 8x8-inch (20x20-cm) cake pans.

Preheat oven to 325°F (160°C).

When dough has risen, take a fist-sized piece and roll out to fit the bottom of one cake pan and ¼ inch (8 mm) up the sides. Take 3 more fist-sized pieces and roll into 3 ropes. Braid the 3 ropes and lay the braid around the inside of the pan on top of the dough. Do the same for the second cake pan.

Filling

Two 2-cup (500-mL) containers dry cottage cheese

4 eggs

2 tsp (10 mL) salt

Pinch of pepper

3 green onions, diced

Mix together well and add to the centre of the dough in the cake pan.

Make two smaller braids and place them on top of the cheese mixture in the shape of an X or T. Trim off extra dough. Bake for ½ hour, then increase oven heat to 350°F (175°C) until lightly browned.

Beans with Garlic

2 cups (475 mL) white beans

1 cup (250 mL) chopped onions

6 garlic cloves, chopped and mashed

2 tbsp (30 mL) oil

2 tsp (10 mL) salt (divided)

1 tsp (5 mL) pepper

Soak beans overnight in water, drain and rinse. In a heavy pot, add the beans and 1 tsp (5 mL) of the salt, cover with water and simmer until tender. Drain the beans and mash them well.

One of her Romanian recipes is Paska, Easter Bread. Families would make the bread and other foods and place them in Easter baskets. Then they would take the bread and baskets to church, where they would be blessed and shared with the congregation at a meal after the Easter service. Linda believes that Ukrainians may also follow this tradition.

—Tom Salley

In a frying pan, sauté the onions with the beans and 1 tsp (5 mL) each salt and pepper.

Mix the chopped and mashed garlic with the oil, then add to the mashed beans.

Beet Rolls

2 cups (475 mL) rice

1 cup (250 mL) chopped onion

¼ cup (60 mL) butter or oil

1 tsp (5 mL) salt

1 tsp (5 mL) pepper

1 pint (475 mL) whipping cream

About 18 fair-sized beet leaves, wilted (but not in water like cabbage)

Cook the rice. Sauté onions in butter or oil and add to rice. Add salt and pepper to taste.

Preheat oven to 325°F (160°C).

Roll rice into the beet leaves as you would for cabbage rolls, tucking in the ends.

Place rolls in a casserole dish. Mix cream with 1 tsp (5 mL) each of salt and pepper and pour over rolls. A bit of water may be added to the cream to thin it. Cover and bake 1½ hours until tender.

Czech

Stuffed Pepper Cups

6 medium green peppers

Salt

1 lb (500 g) ground beef

⅓ cup (80 mL) chopped onion

2 cups (475 mL) stewed tomatoes

1 cup (250 mL) precooked rice

2 tbsp (30 mL) Worcestershire sauce

Salt and pepper to taste

1 cup (250 mL) shredded cheese

Cut the tops off peppers and remove seeds. Precook in boiling, salted water about 5 minutes. Drain. Sprinkle inside with salt.

Brown meat and onions in a large pot. Add tomatoes, rice, Worcestershire sauce, salt and pepper. Cover and simmer. Add cheese.

Stuff peppers with the meat mixture, stand them upright in a baking dish and bake uncovered at 350°F (175°C) for 50 to 55 minutes. This recipe freezes well; freeze before baking.

Olga Slavik

There is a lot of laughter in the Slavik household—and a lot of stories, often accompanied by more laughter at the memories. The Slaviks emigrated from Czech Republic in 1968. There was a new Czech government that was attempting to recreate socialism "with a human face"; however, the Soviet government didn't like this new face, so it sent in the military. Two months later, Olga and her husband, Otto, were in Canada. They said it

was easy to leave. They pretended to go for a holiday to Vienna, and the authorities, who suspected the Slaviks' plans, gave them the holiday visa, as if their attitude was "You are young. There is no future here. You go." They went to Vienna, quickly received permission to immigrate to Canada and ended up in Prince George. They lived there for a number of years before moving to Williams Lake in 1992.

Olga is the cook in the family. She has nourished not only her husband and children, but also many seasonal workers and tourists in the Cariboo Chilcotin. For twelve summers, she cooked in tree-planting camps. Her cooking was very popular, but Olga laughs as she claims she was motivated by fear. "There were so many people in the camp. If I don't put anything on the table, they will beat me up!"

However, her biggest danger came not from the tree planters but from a different hungry eater. Once, while she was preparing breakfast at 4 a.m., a bear was eating peanut butter and cookies just three metres away from where she was cooking. She didn't hear the animal due to the noise of the generator, but when the bear was discovered, Olga tried to protect it. She and the camp manager had different thoughts about it, and unfortunately for the bear, the camp manager won out. The bear's delight in Olga's cooking brought its demise.

Plum Cake

½ cup (125 mL) butter, softened

½ cup (125 mL) + 1 tbsp (15 mL) sugar, divided

2 eggs

1 tsp (5 mL) vanilla

1 cup (250 mL) flour

1 tsp (5 mL) baking powder

¼ tsp (1 mL) salt

3 cups (720 mL) sliced fresh plums

¼ tsp (1 mL) ground cinnamon

In a bowl, cream butter and ½ cup sugar. Add eggs, one at a time, beating well. Add vanilla. Combine flour, baking powder and salt; add to creamed mixture and mix well. Transfer mixture to a greased 9-inch (23-cm) square baking dish. Top with plums. Combine cinnamon and 1 tbsp sugar and sprinkle over plums.

Topping

½ cup (125 mL) flour

¼ cup (60 mL) sugar

¼ cup (60 mL) cold butter, cubed

3 tbsp (45 mL) chopped walnuts, optional

Combine flour, sugar and butter until it resembles coarse crumbs. Stir in walnuts. Sprinkle over top. Bake at 350°F (175°C) for 50 to 55 minutes.

Svíčková

(Pronounced sveetch-kova)

Filet of beef with sour-cream sauce.

Makes 6 servings

3 lbs (1.5 kg) filet of beef or eye of round, rolled and tied securely at 1-inch (2.5-cm) intervals

½ lb (225 g) onions, sliced

1 cup (250 mL) diced celery

⅔ cup (160 mL) diced carrots

1 cup (250 mL) diced parsnips

¼ cup (60 mL) diced bacon

8 peppercorns

4 whole allspice

2 bay leaves

1 tsp (5 mL) salt

Freshly ground black pepper

¼ tsp (1 mL) thyme

1 tbsp (15 mL) melted butter

2 cups (475 mL) beef or chicken stock (+ ½ cup/125 mL if needed), boiled

Preheat oven to 450°F (230°C).

Place the beef in a 4- to 5-quart (4- to 5-L) casserole or saucepan and add the onions, celery, carrots, parsnips, bacon, peppercorns, allspice, bay leaves, salt, a few grindings of pepper, and

Along with their delicious Czech cuisine, the Slaviks now eat a more international diet. Olga says the traditional Czech food tastes good but is usually too sweet or fatty for today's health standards. "People in the past, they work all day in the field, so they have a reason to eat like that."

Olga and Otto are enjoying their retirement in Chimney Valley along with their son, Otto Jr., their large dog, Kira, Rezi the cat, half a dozen sheep and a few colonies of bees. When asked why they stayed in the community, they both reply, "We like it here. This is just perfect."

—Margaret-Anne Enders

Notes

the thyme. Dribble the melted butter evenly over the meat and vegetables. It is customary to marinate the meat in this mixture for at least 24 hours. However, this step may be omitted.

Bake the filet, uncovered, in the middle of the oven for 25 to 30 minutes, or until the vegetables and meat are lightly browned, turning the meat once while cooking.

Lower the temperature to 350°F (175°C). Pour 2 cups (475 mL) of boiled stock into the casserole and bake for 1 hour longer, turning the meat occasionally. Add more stock only if the liquid seems to be cooking away too rapidly. Arrange the finished beef on a platter and keep it warm in a 200°F (95°C) oven while making the sauce.

Sauce

2 cups (475 mL) sour cream

2 tbsp (30 mL) flour

1 tbsp (15 mL) lemon juice

Purée cooked vegetables in a blender; then return them to the casserole and bring to a simmer over medium heat. In a mixing bowl, add 2 tbsp (30 mL) of the puree to the sour cream, then beat in the flour with a wire whisk. Stir the sour cream and puree mixture into the casserole. Cook for 3 or 4 minutes without boiling. Add the lemon juice. Taste for seasoning. Serve the beef sliced and the sauce separately.

Opposite: Heidi Mueller and her husband, Paul Briggs.

Pork Chops Gourmet

4 large pork chops

2 tbsp (30 mL) mustard

1 tsp (5 mL) salt

¼ tsp (1 mL) ground pepper

1 small garlic clove, diced

2 tbsp (30 mL) oil

Mix the mustard, salt, ground pepper and garlic together and brush onto the pork chops.

Heat oil in frying pan and fry the chops on both sides. Then lay them flat in a casserole dish.

Topping

3 cups (720 mL) mushrooms, diced

1 large onion, diced

3 slices of ham, diced

1 tbsp (15 mL) wine or water

Add your favourite spices to taste

Mix all ingredients together and pour over the pork chops.

Sprinkle with 2 tbsp (30 mL) whipped cream and cover with aluminum foil.

Bake for 15 minutes at 400°F (205°C).

Heidi Mueller

Heidi and her husband were vacationing in the Cariboo in the mid-1980s when they fell in love with a beautiful old place on the Fraser River near Soda Creek. Heidi explains that very few people in Switzerland can afford such a beautiful place on the water. The property and a new start in Canada drew them, and by 1988 they were landed immigrants. Heidi and her husband were both excited to become involved in their new way of life in rural Canada. Ten years later they sold their place on the Fraser and moved into Williams Lake. When her husband passed away, Heidi says that's when she really began to learn about living in the wild area we call the Cariboo Chilcotin.

She could have easily returned to Switzerland after her loss, as many people might have, but Heidi stuck it out. She took a job out west at a lodge in the Chilcotin, and there she met her future husband, Paul Briggs, who had come from New York State many years earlier. Paul is an avid hunter and outdoorsman who made his living operating equipment.

Heidi says she learned the true nature of living in this area from Paul. She is proud to have learned how to hunt and fish. Now she can take a freshly killed animal from the forest to the stove. She has learned how to render all the useful parts of an animal's carcass. She also knows the importance of taking care of the wild places where these animals live for the generations to come. She now calls herself a true Canadian because there is nothing more important than getting out into the wilds to enjoy and experience them.

When Heidi lived on the Fraser River, it didn't take long for all in the neighbourhood to discover that she was a fabulous cook. Heidi shares three traditional Swiss recipes: Pork Chops Gourmet, Mousse au Chocolat and Potato Casserole.

—Tom Salley

Mousse au Chocolat

2–3 eggs, whites and yolks separated

½–¾ cup (125 mL–180 mL) sugar

3–4 oz (100 g–120 g) dark chocolate

3–5 tbsp (45–75 mL) warm coffee

1 tsp (5 mL) whipping cream

Combine the egg yolks with the sugar and and mix well.

Break the chocolate into small pieces, add warm coffee to melt the chocolate and then add the egg yolk mix.

Whip the cream and the egg whites.

Gently mix everything together and let stand in the cold. If you mix too vigorously the mixture might separate.

Serve cold.

Potato Casserole

2 lbs (1 kg) uncooked potatoes, peeled and thinly sliced

Pinch of salt, pepper and nutmeg

4–6 small garlic cloves, minced

1 ⅔–2 cups (400–500 mL) whipping cream

Place potato slices flat like shingles in a casserole dish. Sprinkle with salt, pepper, nutmeg and garlic.

Spread whipping cream over the dish.

Bake at 350°F (175°C) for 60 to 70 minutes.

Option: No garlic—add diced onion and bacon, ham or grated cheese.

The kitchen is a country in which there are always discoveries to be made.

—Grimod de la Reynière

Verena Berger

Verena met her husband, Willy, while living in her home country of Switzerland. When Willy left for Canada and began living in Montreal, Verena thought that might be the end of their relationship because Willy had fallen in love with the new country. But they stayed in touch.

Willy apparently kept a warm spot in his heart for Verena because when she expressed an interest in coming to Canada, he invited her to join him in Vancouver. Once she arrived she knew she wanted to stay. This probably had more to do with Willy than the city of Vancouver.

When they decided to tie the knot, they went to Point Barrow, Alaska, for the most unconventional marriage ceremony. Point Barrow lies within the Arctic Circle and is only accessed by plane or barge. Verena says they went to the end of the world for the beginning of their life together.

Swiss

Cheese Soufflé
(Dinner for two)

⅓ cup (80 mL) butter

1 cup (250 mL) white flour

2 cups (475 mL) scalded milk

6 eggs

½ lb (250 g) cheese—spicy Havarti or aged Gouda, grated

Pinch of salt

Preheat oven to 360°F (180°C).

Melt butter in a stainless steel pot over medium heat. Mix in flour until combined with butter, then add hot milk. Keep stirring until the sauce thickens.

Beat each egg individually and add to sauce, stirring with each addition. Add the grated cheese and salt. Keep stirring until the cheese is melted and the contents start to detach from the sides of the pot.

Immediately pour into buttered ovenproof dish and bake for about 30 minutes.

Tomato Salad

2 medium-sized tomatoes, sliced

1–2 green onions, chopped

Balsamic vinegar

Basil

Place the tomato slices accordion-style on a platter. Sprinkle with chopped onions, basil and balsamic vinegar. Serve.

Butter Lettuce with Homemade Dressing

1 butter lettuce

2 tbsp (30 mL) virgin olive oil

2 tbsp (30 mL) white wine vinegar

1 tsp (5 mL) plain yogurt

1 tsp (5 mL) mayonnaise

½ tsp (2.5 mL) Maggi (or soy sauce)

Salt and pepper

Wash and tear lettuce to desired pieces.

In a large bowl, whisk together remaining ingredients. Mix in the greens and serve.

While exploring Canada in their Volkswagen bus they discovered affordable property near Williams Lake. This was something not available to them in Switzerland. In 1980 they moved to the Cariboo where they had purchased ten acres of property in the Miocene area. They were now ready to start a family, and soon Oliver arrived, then Melanie.

Verena loved her new Canadian family and surroundings and the freedom to do as she wished on their little farm. But eventually she gave that up and moved into Williams Lake in the 1990s so her children could have a few more options.

Verena explains that when she grew up in Switzerland, young women were farmed out to other households to learn to cook and clean and become homemakers. This was thought to greatly increase their marriage prospects. Through her mother's mentoring and the home placements she chose, Verena honed her culinary skills.

After her children left home, Verena decided to pursue her lifelong dream of becoming a writer. Not only did she give it her best shot, she is now the published author of *Kool-Aid and Cariboo Stew*, a self-published memoir of her immigrant experiences in Canada. She recently completed an audio version of her book with local music producer Randy Pokeda. You can find both versions of her book at local bookstores or online at www.verenaberger.com.

—Tom Salley

Fruit Salad

1 orange

1 cup (250 mL) green seedless grapes

1 cup (250 mL) purple seedless grapes

1 banana

2 tbsp (30 mL) Kirsch (liqueur)

¼ cup (60 mL) apple juice

Slice fruit into bite-sized pieces, pour liquids over, stir and refrigerate for 2 hours.

Spanish

Gazpacho Soup

Juice of one fresh lemon or 2 tbsp (30 mL) lemon juice concentrate

2 tsp (10 mL) wine vinegar

½ tsp (2.5 mL) Worcestershire sauce

2½ cups (600 mL) canned tomato juice

2 garlic cloves, crushed

3 large tomatoes, peeled and finely chopped

3 inches (8 cm) of long English cucumbers, grated or chopped

2 tbsp (30 mL) finely grated onion

½ green or red pepper, cored, seeded and finely chopped

Salt and pepper to taste

Put the lemon juice, vinegar and Worcestershire sauce in a large mixing bowl. Add the tomato juice and garlic, and mix well.

Stir in the vegetables and mix well. If a smoother soup is preferred, use a blender on low setting. Season to taste. Cover the bowl and chill thoroughly. To serve, put three or four ice cubes in serving bowl and add soup. Garnish with fresh chopped herbs.

A delicious cold soup for hot summer days.

Tony Savile

Tony Savile was born in Yorkshire, England. His father was in the petroleum industry and worked all over the world. This led to the family often moving or travelling to different countries for extended visits. While Tony was growing up, his experiences included stints in the Middle East and East Africa. As he matured and joined the workforce, he began a career in sales that took him from England and into much of Europe. Eventually he was given the opportunity of employment in Montreal, and he arrived in Canada in

1975. He worked in the Montreal and Toronto areas for a few years and became a citizen in 1978. He moved to Vancouver in 1981, where he met his first partner. After the arrival of their two children, Michelle and Victoria, they moved north to Williams Lake where his wife had family. This also facilitated a career change for Tony. He became a cabinetmaker and antique furniture restorer and opened his own shop in Williams Lake. He is now retired but still keeps his hands busy doing a bit of contract woodworking and furniture restoration.

During his time in the Cariboo, Tony found his passion for theatre. He started working on sets for the Williams Lake Studio Theatre and soon discovered he enjoyed all aspects of the theatre, from backstage management to acting and directing. This is still one of his treasured passions, so don't be surprised if you meet him at one of the next productions.

Tony grew up in a small town in England and finds that Williams Lake has that same kind of feel. He loves the friendliness of the Cariboo and is impressed by the level of artistic and technical talent that abounds in the rich culture of the community. Two recipes that Tony shares are Gazpacho Soup and Coq au Vin Blanc (chicken in white wine sauce).

—Tom Salley

Coq au Vin Blanc

(Chicken in white wine sauce)

Chicken pieces (2 thighs, 2 breasts, or smaller pieces)

¼ cup (57 g) butter

2 tbsp (30 mL) olive oil

3–4 thick slices bacon, chopped into 1-inch (2.5-cm) pieces

8 oz (225 g) button onions, peeled, or use chopped onion

2–3 garlic cloves, crushed or finely chopped

1½ cups (350 mL) dry white wine

1½ cups (350 mL) chicken stock

2–3 bay leaves

½ tbsp (7.5 mL) each dry oregano and thyme

¼ tsp (1 mL) fresh ground pepper

Salt to taste

4 oz (125 g) button mushrooms

¼ cup (60 mL) flour

Preheat oven to 325°F (160°C).

Melt half the butter with the oil in the frying pan. Add the bacon and fry until golden brown. Transfer the bacon to an ovenproof casserole dish. Fry the onions and garlic until lightly browned and add to the casserole.

Brown the chicken on all sides and add to the casserole. Remove excess fat from the pan, stir in the white wine and chicken stock and bring to a boil. Pour into the casserole and add the bay leaves, herbs and salt and pepper. Cover tightly and place in a preheated oven for about an hour.

Melt the remaining butter and mix it together with the flour. Whisk into the casserole, add button mushrooms and continue to cook for another 20 to 30 minutes.

Serve with new potatoes, or rice and a vegetable, and accompany with a dry white wine such as Chardonnay or Pinot Grigio.

Notes

Dina (Guilherminia) Goncalves

Dina came from a family in Portugal who owned land. They had olive groves and grew fruits and vegetables. She says that just about everything they ate came from their own gardens and fields. In her village, everyone raised the children, and the community's values were about those families and children. The problem was that Portugal was under fascist rule, and by the age of eighteen Dina knew she wanted more options and a better future than was available in her home country. So with the courage of her youthfulness she immigrated to Canada, leaving her sweetheart, Pedro, behind. Dina had extended family living in Vancouver and they helped her get settled. A year and a half after landing in Vancouver, she

Portuguese Chicken Stew

2 lbs (1 kg) chicken, cut into serving pieces

1½ cups (350 mL) water

½ cup (125 mL) olive oil

1 medium onion, finely chopped

2 garlic cloves, finely chopped

1 very ripe tomato, seeded, peeled and coarsely chopped, or 2 tsp (10 mL) tomato paste

2 bay leaves

1½ tsp (7.5 mL) white pepper

½ tsp (2.5 mL) rosemary

½ cup (125 mL) white wine

1½ tsp (7.5 mL) salt or to taste

Combine all ingredients and simmer for 1½ hours.

Serve with rice or boiled potatoes.

Dina's Portuguese Roasted Potatoes

(Dina's own creation)

6 large potatoes, peeled and quartered

½ tsp (2.5 mL) garlic powder

1½ tsp (7.5 mL) seasoning salt

1 tsp (5 mL) basil

1½ tsp (7.5 mL) dried rosemary

½ tsp (2.5 mL) paprika

½ cup (125 mL) olive or canola oil

½ tsp (2.5 mL) black pepper

1½ tsp (7.5 mL) parsley, finely chopped

Preheat oven to 400°F (205°C).

In a large bowl combine all the ingredients. Mix well to coat potatoes evenly. Place potatoes on cookie sheets. Roast in oven for 1 hour and 15 minutes and serve.

returned to Portugal to marry Pedro Goncalves, a millwright and metal fabricator, and bring him back to Canada, as was their plan. They returned to Vancouver in 1975 and soon started a family with the arrival of their daughter, Christina.

In 1977 they moved to Williams Lake because there were employment options for both of them. They also had family there who could help them until they got their feet on the ground. Pedro worked any job he could find while waiting for his Portuguese millwright ticket to be accepted by Canada. After becoming a ticketed Canadian millwright, finding work in a mill town like Williams Lake was easy. Pedro didn't stop there though. Soon he started his own metal fabricating company called Williams Lake Railings.

In Williams Lake, Dina found some of the same community and family values that she grew up with in her village in Portugal. Although she liked the coast better, Williams Lake was a good place to raise a family. It was a small rural town with good employment opportunities. The people were friendly and there was a real sense of community.

Dina was a working mom and quickly secured employment at Cariboo Memorial Hospital after they arrived. She gave birth to their second child, Suzana, not long after settling in. Now the girls are grown up and Dina retired from Cariboo Memorial Hospital in 2010. When visiting with the Goncalveses you get the feel of a Portuguese home from all of Pedro's outdoor brick and ironwork intermingled with Dina's beautiful gardens.

Dina shares two Portuguese recipes that her mother taught her and one that she created herself.

—Tom Salley

Portuguese Sweet Rice Pudding

2 cups (475 mL) water

Peel of one lemon in large pieces

1 cup (250 mL) short-grain rice

¼ tsp (1 mL) salt

2 cups (475 mL) whole milk, scalded

1½ cups (350 mL) sugar

Cinnamon for decorating

Pour water into a saucepan, add the lemon peel, cover and bring to a boil.

Stir in rice and salt, reduce heat to medium-low, cover and simmer the rice for 20 to 25 minutes.

Add warm milk and stir constantly. When the rice is well cooked, stir in the sugar. Continue cooking and stirring for 5 to 10 minutes. The rice should be very tender. Remove from heat and let it cool.

Remove the lemon peel. Pudding will continue to thicken as it cools. Pour the pudding onto a large, flat serving tray or onto individual flat plates. Take a pinch of ground cinnamon and dust the surface of the rice in a design of your choice.

Italian

Leonora's Spaghetti Sauce

2 tbsp (30 mL) olive oil

1 garlic clove, chopped

½ onion, chopped

1 carrot, chopped

6 tomatoes, chopped

1 tbsp (15 mL) chopped fresh parsley

2 tbsp (30 mL) chopped fresh basil

Cinnamon to taste

Salt and pepper to taste

Heat oil in saucepan. Add garlic and onion and cook until soft and clear. Add chopped carrot and cook another 5 minutes. Add tomatoes and bring to a simmer. Add parsley, basil, cinnamon and salt and pepper to taste. Simmer over medium-low heat for an hour.

Dinner Rolls

1 tbsp (15 mL) yeast

1 tbsp (15 mL) sugar

1 tbsp (15 mL) olive oil

4–6 cups (950 mL–1.4 L) white flour

Zest of one orange

½ tsp (2.5 mL) salt

1 cup (250 mL) lukewarm water (divided)

Dissolve sugar and yeast in ¼ cup (60 mL) of lukewarm water in a large glass or stone-

Cathie Allen

Cathie Allen is all about food. She spends her working days, along with her husband, Rob Borsato, tending a five-acre market garden called Mackin Creek Farm. It's a certified organic, draft-horse-powered farm overlooking the Fraser River just north of Soda Creek. Mackin Creek cuts a deep ravine through the farm.

Rob and Cathie got together in Quesnel about twenty-seven years ago, just before they started their adventures at Mackin Creek. When Cathie first met Rob's Italian mom, Leonora, she was impressed with how good her cooking was, but also how simple it was. She learned that, characteristically, Italian food is all about using fresh, high-quality ingredients, then creatively accenting them with just the right combination of herbs, and cooking it all so as not to lose the flavours and textures of the individual parts.

The Borsatos came from the northeastern part of Italy called the Veneto (near Venice). Both sides of the family left Italy during the stormy political times just prior to the First World War. They independently ended up in the Kootenay area of British Columbia, joining other Italian immigrants in a large community near Trail.

When Rob and Cathie got a chance to visit the Italian home of one of Rob's grandfathers some years ago, they saw that the residents of the area routinely used many of the same vegetables that grow here in the Cariboo. They include broccoli, green beans, salad greens, radicchio, onions, garlic, tomatoes and various herbs.

Cathie's passion for food doesn't stop in the garden. In winter months she lays down the hoe and picks up her watercolours and paintbrush. Many of her art pieces feature the crops they grow or activities in the growing process, such as draft horses working the ground for planting. Additionally, she often shares her recipes with their customers in their weekly Mackin Creek Farm newsletter.

Cathie has picked three of her favourite Italian recipes to share with us.

—Rob Borsato with Tom Salley

Page 109: Cathie Allen and her husband, Rob Borsato, at Mackin Creek Farm.

ware bowl. When yeast has bubbled to double in size, slowly mix in flour half a cup at a time. Add remaining water as needed. When dough is still very wet, add orange zest and salt. Continue mixing in flour until dough is stiff and comes away from the side of the bowl.

Transfer the dough to a flat surface, sprinkling a little flour as you knead the dough. When dough is smooth and elastic, put it back into a bowl greased with olive oil. Let it rise for at least an hour.

Shape dough into rolls on an oiled cookie sheet and let rise for 20 minutes.

Bake in a preheated oven at 400°F (205°C) for 15 to 20 minutes, until golden brown.

Simple Dressing for Green Salad

¼ cup (60 mL) balsamic vinegar

1 tbsp (15 mL) melted honey

1 garlic clove, chopped fine

½ cup (125 mL) olive oil

½ tsp (2.5 mL) Dijon mustard

Mix all ingredients in a jar with a lid. Shake to mix.

Greek

Layered Greek Spanakopita

Inspired by *Cooking and Baking the Greek Way* by Anne Theoharous

2 packages (10 oz/280 g each) frozen chopped spinach

6 tbsp (90 mL) olive oil

6 whole green onions, minced

½–1 lb (250–500 g) feta cheese

12-oz (330-g) container of cottage cheese at room temperature

½ cup (125 mL) finely chopped fresh parsley

⅛ tsp (1 mL) white pepper

2 tsp (10 mL) fresh or dried dill

6 medium eggs, well beaten, at room temperature

1 cup (250 mL) unsalted butter, melted

1 package of phyllo dough

Preheat oven to 325°F (160°C).

Defrost spinach at room temperature and drain.

Heat oil and sauté green onions until soft. Add spinach and simmer until moisture evaporates.

Rinse feta under cold water, drain and crumble it into a large bowl. Mix cottage cheese,

Martine Vitoratos

Kasha and Maia Vitoratos, aged nine and ten, speak French at home with their parents, Martine and Perry. They speak Greek with their grandfather, and Italian with their grandmother, who both live in Quebec.

Kasha and Maia were born and raised in Williams Lake and absolutely love living there. Although their extended family lives on the other side of Canada, being connected to their cultural and family traditions is very much a part of their lives. Every year they celebrate Christmas Eve in the French-Canadian tradition, starting with a fondue, followed by tourtière meat pies served after midnight Mass.

Christmas Day is all about Italy, with a special family recipe of lasagna and sponge cake. On New Year's Day they celebrate their Greek heritage with tzatziki, spanakopita, roasted lamb, Greek salad and more.

Hailing from the very small French-Canadian community of Saguenay–Lac-St-Jean, Quebec, Martine met her husband, Perry, while both were attending university in Montreal. Martine was studying to become a teacher and Perry a dentist. After graduating, Martine saw a small ad in a dental magazine advertising for a dentist in Williams Lake. "Where's that?" asked Perry. Neither of them had ever been to western Canada. In fact, when they journeyed west, it was Martine's first time in an airplane.

They planned to spend four years in Williams Lake, but that was seventeen years ago. Martine and Perry both love outdoor sports and were entranced by the Cariboo's natural beauty. They saw the possibility for a great quality of life.

Martine barely spoke English, and after Montreal the Cariboo was a huge culture shock. They had never seen cowboys or experienced the vast wilderness. Martine chuckles that she learned to speak English by watching television and reading the subtitles. Eventually she taught French Immersion at École Marie Sharpe Elementary School for ten years.

When Perry is not at his dentistry practice he is an avid fisherman and hunter. His mother immigrated with her family to Montreal from Italy when she was four years old. His father was eighteen years old when he emigrated from Greece to Montreal.

Perry's mom is a fantastic Italian cook. She learned how to cook Greek food from a Greek cookbook, and later taught Martine, step by step, all of her favourite recipes. Martine laughs as she explains how her Italian mother-in-law cooks Greek food. "She has taken the Greek recipes and made them her own. She makes her spanakopita just like she is making lasagna. Greek with an Italian twist!" Martine shares a special Vitoratos recipe.

—Marilyn Livingston

parsley, pepper and dill and add to the feta. Whisk eggs well and add them to the mixture. Add spinach and green onions and mix well.

Brush melted butter over sides, corners and bottom of a rectangular pan (a lasagna pan).

Peel off one sheet of phyllo and lay it flat on the bottom of pan. Brush with melted butter. Continue to add sheets of buttered phyllo until there are 7 layers.

Spread cheese mixture over the phyllo and add 3 more buttered sheets. Add more cheese mixture and buttered phyllo until the cheese is used up. Place 3 or 4 buttered sheets to make top layer.

Sprinkle 10 drops of cold water on phyllo so crust will not curl while baking. Using a sharp knife, cut only top layers of phyllo into triangular or square-shaped pieces.

Bake for 45 minutes, or until golden brown.

Bon Appétit!

Martine, Perry, Kasha and Maia Vitoratos.

Hint: Frozen phyllo dough can be bought from most supermarkets, but must be thawed and handled carefully. It can be thawed the night before in the fridge, or before cooking. Allow at least three hours before handling.

Irish

Tea Cake

1¾ cups (415 mL) flour

Pinch of salt

1 tsp (5 mL) baking powder

⅓ cup (80 mL) margarine

½ cup (125 mL) sugar

1 cup (250 mL) sultana raisins or currants

¼ cup (60 mL) candied citrus peel

1 egg plus 1 egg yolk

¾ cup (180 mL) milk

Preheat oven to 375°F (190°C).

Sift together flour, salt and baking powder in a large bowl. Cut margarine into small chunks and rub it into the flour mixture. Add sugar and fruit and mix well.

In a smaller bowl, beat egg and egg yolk and stir in milk. Pour enough egg and milk mixture into the flour to combine into a wet dough.

Put in a well-greased loaf tin and bake for 50 minutes. Leave to cool. Eat when fresh, with butter and jam!

Pauline Robinson

No doubt about it, Pauline Robinson is a true Galway girl. Her dark hair, fair skin, blue eyes and lilting voice tell you right away that she hails from the land of leprechauns and potatoes. And yet, somehow, she made her way from Ireland to the Cariboo, drawn by the lure of adventure and the desire to explore the countryside. Pauline loves being active and you often come upon her pushing her limits cross-country skiing, running and mountain-biking. She's especially keen on the Canadian winter, playing hockey at Scout Island when the ice is clear. "It's beautiful in the Cariboo with the blue skies. You just want to be outside."

Although she spent her childhood in a different land, Pauline shares a history that is familiar to many of the folks around the Cariboo Chilcotin who grew up pioneering on the land. The farm that her kith and kin call home has been in her family for several generations. They raise sheep, pigs, dairy and beef cows, and grow crops of barley. Pauline recalls the work hours were long—seven days a week. There were no luxuries, but always enough fresh farm food to go around.

Meals in the Robinson household were fairly simple: meat, vegetables and potatoes, and most of it produced right on their own farm. "No spices, no pasta, no rice." You can see Pauline's mouth water as she talks about potatoes. They were a daily

Beef and Guinness Stew

2½ lbs (1.25 kg) stewing steak, cut into chunks

¼ cup (60 mL) flour

5 tbsp (75 mL) vegetable oil

1 large onion, chopped

1 cup (250 mL) Guinness beer

1½ cups (350 mL) beef or vegetable stock

Worcestershire sauce to taste

Salt and pepper to taste

1½ lbs (750 g) potatoes, peeled and cut into chunks

1 lb (500 g) carrots, peeled and cut into chunks

8 oz (225 g) frozen peas

Coat the meat with the flour.

Heat the oil in a large saucepan. Add the pieces of meat a few at a time and cook until brown on all sides. Remove as they brown and reduce the heat. Add the onion to the remaining oil in the pan and cook until almost tender. Stir in any reserved flour. Return the meat to the pan.

Gradually stir in the Guinness and stock, Worcestershire sauce, salt and pepper and cook, stirring, until slightly thickened. Bring to a boil. Reduce the heat, cover and simmer for 2½ hours until almost tender.

Add the potatoes and carrots. Stir well and

bring back to a boil. Reduce the heat, cover and simmer for 20 minutes.

Stir in the frozen peas and simmer for a further 5 to 10 minutes until the beef and all the vegetables are tender.

Scones

3½ cups (845 mL) flour

1 tsp (5 mL) baking powder

½ tsp (2.5 mL) salt

¼ cup (60 mL) margarine or butter

⅓ cup (80 mL) coconut

⅓ cup (80 mL) sugar

1 egg

¾ cup (180 mL) fresh milk

Preheat oven to 425°F (220°C).

In a large bowl, sift together flour, baking powder and salt. Add margarine and rub into the flour with fingertips until it resembles bread crumbs. Add the coconut and the sugar and mix well.

In a smaller bowl, beat the egg slightly, add the milk and beat until blended.

Add the beaten egg and milk to the flour mixture and combine into a dough-like form. Roll out dough on a floured surface with a rolling pin until it is about ½ inch (1.25 cm) thick and cut with fluted round cutter.

Place the scones on a greased cookie sheet. Bake for 15 to 20 minutes until golden brown.

staple—mashed (with boiling milk, spring onions and butter), boiled, steamed, roasted, fried, potato salad—sometimes two different ways in the same meal, and always with loads of butter.

Because the savoury food was fairly plain, Pauline describes her parents as being rather skeptical of what she calls "fancy food." However, Pauline's eyes twinkle when she describes her dad's sweet tooth and the treats her mammy would bake in their woodstove after the long day of work on the farm: apple tarts, rhubarb tarts, scones and currant cake. There were sweets after every meal and a special dessert on Sundays.

While beef and Guinness stew, scones and tea cake are not the daily helpings on her plate these days, they are the dishes that bring to her a sense of home. Pauline's tastes are now more experimental but she still follows her mam's tradition of cooking from scratch using fresh local ingredients.

And how does Pauline describe her relationship to food? "I love food! I'm a total foodie."

—Margaret-Anne Enders

Mary Krajczar

Mary was a midwife in Scotland when she decided to immigrate to Canada in 1960. She arrived in Victoria, BC, at the age of twenty-six and soon met Erno Krajczar, a Hungarian student who had fled the Soviet invasion during the 1956 Hungarian revolution. Within two years of Mary's arrival they were married. The newlyweds moved to Prince Rupert and then in 1972 to Williams Lake, where Erno found an engineering position with the BC Forest Service. During that time the Krajczars added two new members to their family, Heather and Keroy, and Mary had her own career as a nurse. She worked in a spectrum of departments in the Cariboo Memorial Hospital, from maternity to dialysis and the diabetes clinics.

Erno, Mary and the children always enjoyed Williams Lake and the Cariboo for the wide-open spaces, fishing, camping and natural wonders. Mary and Erno are both retired now, but it is easy to see how their contribution to the community has been crucial in building the community of Williams Lake and Canada in general.

Some of Mary's recipes were passed down to her through three generations. She started sharing her recipes with the world a few years ago on YouTube. To view these, simply Google Mary's Scottish Shortbread or Mary's Bramble Jam. Enjoy!

—Tom Salley

Mary's Scottish Shortbread

1 lb (475 mL) soft butter

1 cup (250 mL) berry sugar

1 cup (250 mL) rice flour

3¼ cups (780 mL) wheat flour

Preheat oven to 300°F (150°C).

Mash and mix butter and sugar together thoroughly. Gradually mix in the rice and wheat flour, kneading with your hands. Roll out with a rolling pin. Cut out shortbread rounds with a glass or into whatever shape you like. Place on cookie sheets and bake in oven for 30 minutes. Cool shortbread on a rack. Serve and eat or store by freezing.

Mary's Scottish Cheese Scones

2 cups (475 mL) flour (any kind)

1 egg, beaten (save a bit to paint tops of scones)

¼ cup (60 mL) butter

3 tsp (15 mL) baking powder

Pinch of sugar

1 cup (250 mL) milk or buttermilk

Squirt of lemon juice

1 cup (250 mL) grated cheese (save a bit for tops of scones)

Preheat oven to 425°F (220°C).

Mix all ingredients together; knead and work well. Squash the dough ball down to about 1 inch (2.5 cm) thick on a floured board or counter. Cut scones out with a glass and place on a cookie sheet. With pastry brush, paint the tops of the scones with the reserved egg. Sprinkle reserved cheese on scones. Place in preheated oven and bake for 15 minutes. Cool and serve.

Mary's Bramble Jam

4 cups (950 mL) blackberries

4 cups (950 mL) sugar

1 packet liquid Certo

1 tsp (5 mL) butter

1 tbsp (15 mL) lemon juice

Put the berries and sugar in a pot and mix them, mashing the berries well. Turn heat on low to medium until the sugar has melted and the berries are well mashed. Bring to a full boil for 1 minute. Take the pan off the heat and add Certo, butter and lemon juice and stir constantly for 5 minutes (otherwise juice will rise to the top of the jar).

Pour jam into hot jars leaving ¼ inch (1.5 cm) of headspace. Screw on hot lid and band until finger tight. Place jars in a water bath and cover completely with water. Cook for 15 minutes at a full boil.

Notes

My grandma, Esme Byers, was proud of her Scottish heritage and loved to say this grace at special family dinners.

—Margaret-Anne Enders

Some hae meat and canna eat,
And some wad eat that want it,
But we hae meat and we can eat,
And sae the Lord be thankit.

—Robert Burns

Tastes

of

Asia

Lubna Khan

In Pakistan it has been the long-standing tradition that only family takes care of the children (not babysitters). When Lubna's sister married an American and moved to the US, it raised the question of who would help with the children. The Khans decided that by following their daughter they could better the family's options and stay close for the children. So in the mid-1990s the family started immigrating to Chicago from Pakistan. Lubna moved to Chicago in 2001. She had already obtained a master's degree from the University of Karachi and a professional

Chana Chaat
(Chickpea snack)

Chana means "chickpea." Chana Chaat is a very popular street food in Pakistan.

1 small sweet onion, diced

4 medium-sized potatoes, boiled and diced

2 medium-sized tomatoes, diced

2 cups (475 mL) boiled or canned chickpeas

Big bunch of cilantro, chopped

1–2 green peppers (jalapeño), chopped

1 large lime

1 tbsp (15 mL) or more chaat masala*

½ cup (125 mL) tamarind sauce/chutney*

Mix onion, potatoes, tomatoes, chickpeas, cilantro and green peppers in a large bowl. Squeeze the whole lime over the vegetables and mix again. Add chaat masala and the tamarind chutney. Mix everything again and taste; add more chaat masala if you want more spice.

* Chaat masala and tamarind sauce/chutney are available in the ethnic food section of Save-On Foods in Vancouver. Chana Chaat gets a lot of flavour from the tamarind sauce/chutney, so it's worth the effort of finding it the next time you visit the big city.

Mango Lassi

(Mango-yogurt drink)

Mango Lassi is the perfect summer drink, but it's not a crime to make it in winter.

2 large mangoes, peeled and diced

1½ cups (350 mL) plain yogurt

½ cup (125 mL) milk

⅛ tsp (0.5 mL) salt

2 tbsp (30 mL) sugar

1–2 cups (250–475 mL) crushed ice or ice cubes

Put diced mangoes, yogurt, milk, salt and sugar in a blender and blend it well. Taste for sweetness and add more sugar if desired. Add more yogurt if you like it tangy.

Add crushed ice or ice cubes and blend again.

Substitue 1 or 1⅓ cups (250–325mL) of cold water for the ice if you don't want it too cold! Blend as you would for ice.

Right: Lubna with her mother, Zebun Nisa.

master's degree in geo-information management from the ITC faculty of University of Twente in Enschede, Netherlands.

Although she liked Chicago and felt at home there, Lubna had heard of the legendary beauty of BC, its mountains, forests and wildlife. When a position opened up in Williams Lake for a geographical information system technician with the BC Ministry of Forestry, she applied and got the job. The employment offered her the opportunity to explore areas and lifestyles and engage in activities that she didn't know she could ever experience. She has since become a Canadian citizen, an avid ice fisher, a member of the Williams Lake Field Naturalist Club and has engaged in nature study. In addition, she occasionally likes to paint and draw portraits. Through the Williams Lake Art Society she was able to display her work in a show the art society sponsored in June 2012.

Lubna's mother was known to be a great cook, so much so that the family would pass up opportunities to dine out whenever Lubna's mom was cooking. Her mother wanted Lubna to focus on education and never mentored her in the culinary arts of Pakistani cuisine. When Lubna came to Williams Lake it did not take long for her to tire of eating hot dogs and to realize she had to learn to cook. She started getting help from her mother over the phone and the internet. Her mother would pass on the recipes, tricks and secrets that always kept the family coming back for more. From there Lubna began to broaden her menu and eat much better because now food relates to family and culture, as it should.

—Tom Salley

Lubna's mother, Zebun Nisa, with Lubna's young niece, Marjina.

Chicken Curry with Turnips

Makes 5 to 7 servings

Whole chicken cut into pieces, skin removed

2 tbsp (30 mL) vegetable oil

1 large onion, thinly sliced

Ginger, 2-inch (5-cm) piece, crushed and diced

5–7 crushed garlic cloves

2 tsp (10 mL) ground coriander

¼ tsp (1 mL) turmeric

½ tsp (2.5 mL) red chili powder

¼ tsp (1 mL) garam masala

1 tbsp (15 mL) water

4 medium-sized turnips, peeled and diced

2 medium-sized tomatoes, diced

Salt to taste

1 bunch cilantro, chopped

1 jalapeño pepper, chopped

Heat oil in a large pan on medium. Sauté onions until soft. Add ginger and garlic and stir for 1 minute. Add coriander, turmeric, red chili powder, garam masala and a tablespoon of water and mix well for 1 minute.

Add chicken pieces, coating them on all sides with the onion and spices, and stir until chicken becomes opaque.

Cover the pan and let cook for 5 to 6 minutes.

In a separate pot, boil turnips. While turnips cook, add diced tomatoes to the chicken and mix well. Cover pan and let cook for a further 5 to 6 minutes. Add salt and cook for 5 minutes more.

Drain turnips and add to chicken. Mix well and season to taste.

Lower heat and cook, covered, for 10 to 15 minutes. Add chopped cilantro and jalapeño pepper 5 minutes before serving.

Serve with roti, pita or boiled rice.

Hint: Turnips can be replaced by cauliflower, potatoes, eggplant or zucchini, in which case the vegetables need not be boiled.

Jasbir Dherari

Jasbir Dherari grew up in India. Her father was a tailor and made men's suits and beautiful traditional women's outfits. As a child, Jasbir did not have television or radio and spent many hours in the kitchen cooking with her mother and all of the other women. This was the beginning of a lifelong passion.

Following tradition, a marriage was arranged to her husband, Gurtej Dherari, whom she now describes as her best friend. They were married in India in January 1978, and the couple arrived in Williams Lake that spring. Since then, many other family members have also moved from India to start new lives. Jasbir and Gurtej's three children were all born and raised in Williams Lake. The Dheraris are

Indian/Punjabi

Vegetable Pakoras
(Indian fritters)

1 cup (250 mL) chickpea flour

1 tsp (5 mL) garam masala

1 tsp (5 mL) salt

1 tsp (5 mL) cayenne pepper

½ tsp (2.5 mL) ground coriander

¾ cup (180 mL) water

1 cup (250 mL) cauliflower florets

½ cup (125 mL) sliced potatoes

3 cups (720 mL) vegetable oil for deep-frying

Sift the chickpea flour into a mixing bowl. Mix in the garam masala, salt, cayenne pepper and coriander.

Make a well in the centre of the flour. Gradually pour the water into the well and mix to form a thick, smooth batter.

Heat oil in a saucepan on medium-high heat.

Coat the cauliflower and potatoes in the batter and deep-fry them in small batches until golden brown, about 4 to 5 minutes. Drain on paper towels before serving.

Left: Jasbir and Gurtej were married in India in 1978 and arrived in Williams Lake that same year.

Kheer
(Rice pudding)

¼ cup (60 mL) long-grained rice, washed and drained

4–5 cups (1–1.2 L) milk

1 tbsp (15 mL) skinned, chopped pistachio nuts

1 tbsp (15 mL) raisins (optional)

2–3 tbsp (30–45 mL) sugar, or as desired

In a saucepan on medium heat, bring the rice and milk to a boil, and then simmer gently until the rice is soft and the grains start to break up.

Add pistachios and raisins and simmer for 3 to 4 minutes.

Add the sugar and stir until completely dissolved.

Remove the rice kheer from the heat and serve either warm or chilled.

Maseu

1 cup (250 mL) homogenized milk

4 cups (950 mL) ghee (clarified butter)

4 cups (950 mL) granulated sugar

2 cups (475 mL) chickpea flour

Pour milk into a large saucepan and add the

now proud grandparents with a grandson and a granddaughter.

Being a young bride and only knowing traditional Indian relationships, Jasbir discovered new-found freedoms in Canada. Many immigrants, especially women, are surprised at the number of choices they have in Canada. "We are happy; this has been a blessing," Jasbir says.

Following in her father's footsteps, Jasbir started sewing Indian outfits. Various women will purchase fabric and drop it off for her to sew. She has also been employed at Ken's Restaurant for nineteen years as cook.

Staying true to her roots, Jasbir has been very involved with the Guru Nanak Sikh Temple. Every Sunday she and the other women dress in traditional attire and prepare a delicious meal for members of the congregation. In addition, Jasbir prepares food for weddings and other ceremonies celebrated at the temple.

When asked if it is difficult to find the Indian spices and ingredients, she says not anymore, but at one time they had to buy their specialty foods in Vancouver. Jasbir has a great respect and appreciation for food. "We appreciate what we are given."

—Marilyn Livingston

ghee, sugar and chickpea flour. Cook on high heat while stirring vigorously.

Turn the temperature down to medium and keep stirring for about 20 to 25 minutes.

Pour the mixture onto a cookie sheet and spread evenly.

Once the mixture cools, cut it into pieces, eat and enjoy.

Chocolate Barfi

(Indian cheesecake)

¾ cup (180 mL) all-purpose flour (maida)

4½ cups (1 L) granulated sugar

3 cups (720 mL) condensed milk

3 tsp (15 mL) cocoa powder

2 tbsp (45 mL) ghee (clarified butter)

2 cups (475 mL) unsalted butter

Over medium heat, mix all the ingredients in a saucepan and stir constantly until holes start appearing and the mixture begins to froth up.

Pour mixture onto a greased cookie sheet.

When cooled, cut into squares and eat.

Breads and Fillings

The combination of bread and savoury filling seems almost universal among cultures. Tacos and burritos, falafels, donairs, gyozas, perogies, calzone, even hotdogs and hamburgers, are all based on this simple concept. Granted there is wide variation between them, but they are culinary relations. And it is interesting that *Spicing Up The Cariboo* includes several such cousins: Thai spring roll, Estonian pirukad, samosas and pakoras from India, Polish nalesniki, and the papa rellena from Peru. Also included are recipes for Secwepemc bannock, and Honduran tortillas, which can compliment any number of dishes with various meats, fish, or vegetarian ingredients.

—Christian Petersen

Indian/Punjabi

Potato Vegetable Samosas

Dough

2 cups (475 mL) all-purpose flour

½ tsp (2.5 mL) salt

2 tbsp (30 mL) vegetable oil

¾ cup (180 mL) warm water

Combine flour and salt. Stir in oil and then stir in warm water. Turn dough out onto a lightly floured surface and knead until dough is elastic, for about 5 minutes. Cover and set aside while preparing the samosa filling.

Filling

2½ cups (600 mL) Yukon Gold potatoes, peeled and diced into ½-inch (1.25-cm) pieces

1 tbsp (15 mL) fennel seeds

1 tbsp (15 mL) cumin seeds

2 tsp (10 mL) coriander seeds

3 tbsp (45 mL) vegetable oil

½ cup (125 mL) finely diced onions

2 garlic cloves, minced

1 inch (2.5 cm) fresh ginger, peeled and grated

1 package (1 lb/500 g) frozen chopped spinach, thawed, with excess juices squeezed out

½ cup (125 mL) frozen peas, thawed

Salt and pepper

Sharon Rathor

Sharon Rathor still remembers the first dish she learned to make. It was corn flour bread, or roti as many call it. It happened when she was a girl of eight, back in the Punjab in Northern India. She was hungry, and while she was snooping around the food bins, she accidentally knocked over the corn flour tin. The heavy tin fell on her foot—leaving a scar that she has to this day—and corn flour was scattered everywhere. Her grandmother came running at the noise of the tin dropping and Sharon crying. After a good scolding for wasting so much flour, her grandmother asked her what she wanted to eat. When Sharon replied that she wanted corn flour bread, her grandmother said, "Okay I'll teach you how to make it." Thus began the special memory of making roti with her grandmother.

When Sharon was ten years old, her family moved to Canada, stopping for a short time in Nanaimo and then moving up to Williams Lake where her father had been offered a job. Sharon recalls that it was a difficult transition, with such a different culture and cuisine. As well, she was

Boil potatoes, uncovered, in salt water until tender. Then drain well and set aside.

In a large saucepan, toast fennel, cumin and coriander seeds for 2 minutes, until fragrant. Add oil, then onion, and fry for 4 minutes, until onion is translucent. Add garlic and ginger and fry 1 minute more. Stir in spinach, peas and cooked potatoes, mashing lightly to combine and warm, then season to taste. Leave filling to cool.

Assembly

Oil for frying

To assemble samosas, divide dough into 12 equal portions and shape each portion into a ball. On a lightly floured surface, roll out 1 ball into a 6-inch (15-cm) circle. Cut circle in half and fold each corner of the semicircle towards the middle, overlapping a bit. It should resemble a triangle. Pinch edges of triangle to seal, leaving rounded side open. Hold triangle in your hand with open side facing up and let dough fall open to make a cone. Fill cone with approximately 2 tbsp (30 mL) potato mixture, then pinch along rounded side to seal.

Repeat with remaining dough and filling. Cover and chill samosas until ready to cook.

Fill a pot with 2 inches (5 cm) of oil, making sure oil fills pot not more than halfway, and heat to 350°F (175°C). With tongs, place samosas in oil, leaving an inch between them, and cook until golden brown, about 4 minutes. Turn and cook the other side until brown, then remove onto a plate lined with paper towels to drain.

Samosas can be served warm or at room temperature with ketchup.

Naan Bread

Makes 9 pieces

3½ cups (450 g) plain flour

½ tsp (2.5 mL) salt

1 tsp (5 mL) baking powder

2 tsp (10 mL) sugar

2 tsp (10 mL) active dry yeast

⅔ cup (160 mL) warm milk,

2–3 tbsp (30–45 mL) vegetable oil (plus ¼ tsp/1 mL for bowl)

⅔ cup (160 mL) plain yogurt, lightly beaten

1 egg, lightly beaten

Melted butter (to brush dough)

Fresh chopped cilantro

Sift the flour, salt, baking powder and sugar into a bowl. Add the yeast. Pour in the heated milk, oil, yogurt and beaten egg and mix together to form a ball of dough.

Place the dough on a clean surface and knead for 10 minutes or more, until it is smooth.

Pour about ¼ tsp (1 mL) oil into a large bowl

called names by the children at school. . After a while, she got used to the community there and Williams Lake became home.

When Sharon was eighteen years old, she sponsored Surinderpal, her soon-to-be husband, to come over from India. Surinderpal's cousin was married to Sharon's sister and so the family arranged the match. The young couple was married in Williams Lake and soon started their own family. Over the years, they have gathered their family close, with many relatives living on the same block.

Sharon has been quite involved with the Indo-Canadian community. She goes to the Guru Nanak Sikh Temple to pray and, before an injured knee prevented her from getting around, she used to help prepare the lunch that is offered each week. At one time there were over four hundred Sikh families in the area, and Sharon

loved when people would just drop in for a visit or stop and say hello as they were walking by. She was always making tea, making food and sharing her home and hospitality.

Preparing food has always been a joy for Sharon. In her working years, she was employed in the kitchen at Cariboo Lodge and cooked for many of the restaurants in town. Now she cooks for herself and Surinderpal—and any of their children or grandchildren who happen to be around. She is a typical grandmother who loves her grandchildren—and loves to spoil them. And when she isn't cooking or at the temple, she is watching East Indian soap operas. "I'm crazy for them!" she laughs.

—Margaret-Anne Enders

Page 129: Sharon, Surinderpal, and their family.

and roll the ball of dough in it.

Cover the bowl and set aside in a warm place for the yeast to do its job. This will take approximately an hour or until the dough has doubled in size.

Preheat oven to 450°F (230°C). Place a heavy baking tray in the oven to heat.

Punch down the dough and knead it again. Divide into 9 equal balls.

While working on 1 ball, keep the remaining balls covered. Flatten the ball, using your hands or rolling pin, into an oval about 6 inches (15 cm) in length by 5 inches (12 cm) in width. Brush the top with melted butter (and sprinkle with minced garlic if you like).

Remove the hot baking tray from the oven, grease it well with butter or oil and place the naan on it. You can cook up to 4 naans on one tray.

Put the tray in the oven on the top rack for 2 to 3 minutes. It should puff up and brown slightly. Keep an eye on it.

Once it's puffed up and browned on one side, flip the naan and put it back into the oven for another 1 to 2 minutes until the top of the naan is golden brown.

Naan is best served hot and sprinkled with some fresh cilantro.

Rajma

(Kidney beans)

1 cup rajma (red kidney beans), dry

1 onion, diced

1 tomato, diced

1 green chili, diced

4–5 garlic cloves, minced

1-inch (2.5 cm) ginger, grated or minced

3 tbsp (45 mL) vegetable oil

1 tsp (5 mL) red chili powder

½ tsp (2.5 mL) turmeric

1 tsp (5 mL) ground coriander

1 tsp (5 mL) garam masala

Salt to taste

Water

Chopped cilantro for garnish

Wash beans by rubbing with hands, changing water 3 to 4 times. Cover beans in water with 2 inches (5 cm) of water above the beans. Soak in water overnight, or minimum of 8 to 9 hours. Cook beans for a couple of hours until soft, but not mushy, or use a pressure cooker for shorter time.

Pulse diced onion, tomato and green chili in a food processor and mix with garlic and ginger to make a paste.

Notes

Heat oil in a pan. Add the paste and fry on medium heat until golden brown and the oil separates.

Add chili powder, turmeric, coriander, garam masala and salt. Mix well. Fry for 2 to 3 minutes.

Add enough water to make a thick gravy and bring to a boil. Add cooked beans with their liquid. Stir well and cook over medium heat for 5 to 7 minutes. Garnish with cilantro and serve hot.

Bengali

Bengali Fish Curry

2 lbs (1 kg) bass fillets, cut into chunks

2 tbsp (30 mL) vegetable oil

1 tsp (5 mL) cumin seeds

1 medium-sized onion, finely chopped

1 tbsp (15 mL) 1:1 ratio ginger/garlic paste

½ tsp (2.5 mL) coriander powder

½ tsp (2.5 mL) turmeric powder

1 tsp (5 mL) chili powder

½ tsp (2.5 mL) ground nutmeg

1 tsp (5 mL) ground black pepper

1 tsp (5 mL) ground cumin

1 medium-sized ripe tomato, finely chopped

1 cup (250 mL) water

1 green chili pepper (optional)

¼ bunch fresh cilantro, finely chopped

2 bunches green onions, finely chopped

Salt to taste

In a wok heat the vegetable oil and sauté cumin seeds. When the cumin turns golden brown, add the onion and fry for 1 to 1½ minutes until onion turns golden brown.

Add the ginger/garlic paste and continue frying for another minute or until the mix turns nearly dark brown.

Muhammed Sabur and Shabnam Shayla

"Eat some more please." If you ever dine at Sabur and Shabnam's home, you will hear these words. Not just once, as a polite offer for a second helping, but many times, even after multiple plates of food. In fact, "dinner" is not a suitable word for a meal there—the only word that fits is "feast."

Sabur and Shabnam come from Bangladesh but arrived fifteen years apart. Sabur left Bangladesh in 1985 to pursue higher education in Thailand and Ireland. He completed his Ph.D. in engineering hydrology in Edmonton and worked for a time in Prince George before settling in Williams Lake. He bought a home and planted a big, beautiful garden full of lush flowers and many kinds of vegetables. In 2000, Sabur returned to Bangladesh in search of a suitable marriage.

Shabnam grew up in a village just a couple of miles away from the small farm where Sabur was raised. Shabnam shared her family's belief in arranged marriages, but one had not been arranged for her yet. Upon hearing that Sabur was in Bangladesh looking for a bride, she asked, "What about me?" However, her family said they were not planning a marriage for her right then. But Shabnam was insistent and finally her parents agreed to let them meet. So they met, and one week later they were married. Not a typical arranged marriage, but not a love marriage either. As is the hope with arranged marriages, the

Add the powdered spices and mix thoroughly. Continue frying for another 5 to 10 seconds.

Add the tomato, turn down the heat and continue frying until the tomato virtually blends with the mix and forms a paste; then add a cup of water and bring to a boil.

Add the fish, green chili, cilantro and green onion.

Cook for 5 to 10 minutes or until the fish is thoroughly cooked.

Add salt to taste. Remove from heat and serve warm with basmati rice.

Left: Sabur, Syrus, Shannon and Shabnam.

Bengali Fish Cakes

6 medium potatoes

4 cans or equivalent weight of fish, canned in water, not oil

1 bunch green onions, finely chopped

¼ bunch fresh cilantro, finely chopped

2 garlic cloves, minced

2–3 tbsp (30–45 mL) fresh minced ginger

1 green chili pepper, minced (optional)

4–5 egg whites

1½–2 cups (350–475 mL) bread crumbs

Salt to taste

Oil for deep-frying

Boil potatoes until cooked. Drain and mash.

Drain canned fish.

Combine potatoes, fish and next five ingredients. Mix well. Add salt to taste.

Make patties and dip them into egg white and then carefully roll in bread crumbs until completely covered. Deep-fry in hot oil, turning to brown, and cook evenly. If patties darken too quickly, turn heat down so inside cooks. Patties can be shallow-fried, but they might not hold together as well.

Remove with slotted spoon and put into bowl lined with paper towel to absorb excess oil.

Hint: These patties can be made with cooked ground meat instead of fish.

love did grow. As Shabnam says, "I think my dream came true."

Sabur returned to Williams Lake and waited for Shabnam to arrive. It took three years for the immigration process to be completed, but finally she made it to Canada. The weather was quite a shock. She arrived on the evening of June 22. On June 23 when she went outside, she was fully prepared for the cold—in a snowsuit, mittens, gloves, hat and boots. She laughs and says, "I hid when I saw the neighbours in bathing suits." After twelve years in Williams Lake, Shabnam is comfortable here. She and Sabur are happy and they have two lovely children, Shannon and Syrus. However her home country and family are alive in her heart: "Canada is a beautiful country, but deep inside I dream of Bangladesh."

Both Sabur and Shabnam are fabulous cooks. They still cook many dishes that are staples in the Bengali diet: fish, lentils, eggs and rice. Sabur does most of the cooking. Shabnam laughs and says, "He likes his own food best." But when Shabnam serves up her dishes for Eid, the Muslim holiday that marks the end of Ramadan, the month of fasting, it is clear that they both have great talents in the kitchen.

— Margaret-Anne Enders

Muhammed Sabur and Shabnam Shayla

Practice makes perfect, so practise,
practise, practise!

—*Sabur*

Daal

(Shabnam's recipe)

½ cup (125 mL) red lentils or mixed lentils

2 cups (475 ml) water

½–1 tsp (2.5–5 mL) salt

Oil for frying

2 garlic cloves

¼ tsp (1 mL) cumin seed

1–2 dried red or green chilies

Pinch fenugreek seeds (optional)

Pinch turmeric

Fresh herbs—dill, cilantro or fenugreek leaves

Rinse and drain lentils and put in a pot with water and salt. Bring to a boil. Simmer for 20 minutes (or 30 if using mixed lentils).

When lentils are almost cooked, heat oil in frying pan. Add garlic and sauté until golden. Add cumin seed, chilies, fenugreek and turmeric. Be careful not to burn the spices. Immediately add the cooked lentils. Cook for another 5 minutes.

Flavour with fresh herbs—dill is popular in Bangladesh.

Sri Lankan

Kiri Bath
(Milk rice)

1 cup (250 mL) white or basmati rice

2 cups (475 mL) water

1 cup (250 mL) thick coconut milk

Salt to taste

Put rice and water in a pot, cover and cook on medium heat. When the rice is almost done, mix the salt with the coconut milk and add to the rice. Stir well and cook on low heat until the rice is well cooked. Put the hot milk rice on a platter or tray. Using a spatula, flatten the rice evenly. Cut into squares or diamonds while hot.

Serve with Chili Sambol, honey, palm syrup or sugar.

Ala Hodi
(White potato curry)

½ lb (250 g) whole potatoes, skin on

2 cloves garlic, sliced

2 green chilies, sliced

½ small onion, chopped

½ tsp (2.5 mL) curry powder

½ tsp (2.5 mL) turmeric powder (*kaha*)

½ tsp (2.5 mL) fenugreek seeds (*uluhall*)

Kusum Wijesekera

There are not many young families that retire and then come to Canada, but for Kusum and Nihal Wijesekera, that was the way it happened. They both worked for the Sri Lankan government, Kusum as a high school math and science teacher, and Nihal as a regional superintendent of the survey and geographic information system (GIS).

After working for twenty years, they were both eligible for retirement, so they applied and then proceeded to move to Canada with their son, Chamath. The retirement, however, was short-lived—and was never the plan anyway. They wanted to come to Canada to give Chamath more educational opportunities, and Nihal was interested in working with GIS systems in this country. After a short stint in Calgary, they moved to Williams Lake where Nihal got a job as a GIS technologist with the Cariboo Regional District.

Kusum still has a connection to the classroom and helps out as a parent-volunteer with Chamath's class when needed. Chamath is happy for the opportunities he has here and loves school and his Grade 6 class, especially swimming lessons and the regular pizza and hot dog days.

The Wijesekeras' sense of adventure has kept the family busy since coming to Canada. They share a great curiosity about landscape and culture and enjoy attending community events and celebrations. They also continue to practise their Buddhist faith and celebrate Buddhist and Sri Lankan holidays. Nihal and Chamath insist that the travelling they have done is their favourite part about living in Canada. Kusum is not so selective.

Curry leaves (*karapincha*) (optional)

1 tsp (5 mL) Maldive fish (*Umbalakada*)*

2 cups (475 mL) thin coconut milk

Salt to taste

Boil the potatoes. Peel and cut into medium-sized chunks and set aside.

Put all the ingredients, except the potatoes and curry leaves (if using), into a pan and mix well over medium heat, stirring constantly until bubbling. Add the potato chunks and curry leaves and cook until potatoes are heated through.

Serve with plain rice, fried rice, noodles, or with bread.

*Maldive fish or *Umbalakada* are dried tuna flakes made in the Maldive Islands. Thurga Trading Co. on Fraser Street in Vancouver carries these, as well as other Sri Lankan foods.

Left: Nihal, Kusum and Chamath.

Chili Sambol

(Lunu miris)

1 medium onion, minced

1 tbsp (15 mL) chili powder

½ tbsp (7.5 mL) salt

1 tbsp (15 mL) Maldive fish (*Umbalakada*)

Juice of ½ lime or lemon

Place all ingredients, except the lime or lemon juice, in a food processor and grind slightly or use a mortar and pestle. Remove to small bowl and add the lime or lemon juice and mix well.

Serve with Kiri Bath, boiled sweet or white potatoes, roti or pita.

Thousands of candles can be lit from a single candle, and the life of the candle will not be shortened. Happiness never decreases by being shared.

—*Buddha*

"I like everything," she says with a smile.

Kusum and her family have maintained a connection to their heritage through their food. In Sri Lanka, meals are a sensory experience. Traditionally, Sri Lankans eat with their hands, so they experience the texture of the food with their fingers, not just their mouths. Vegetables, prepared on their own with spices, are the major ingredients of Sri Lankan food. Fish, meat and beans or lentils are served as protein. There are a great many trees with edible leaves, so people go out to their gardens, pick the leaves and then cook them. Coconut is also one of the main ingredients of the meal. In Sri Lanka, fresh coconut is plentiful, but Kusum finds that she can still make traditional recipes using desiccated coconut and canned coconut milk. Another local treat is palm sugar, made from the palm flower's nectar. They also flavour many of their dishes with Maldive fish, dried tuna flakes imported from the Maldives. Nihal points out that one cannot speak of Sri Lankan cuisine without mentioning that Ceylon tea is the "best tea in the world."

—Margaret-Anne Enders

Esther Wong

Esther completed a degree in sociology at the University of Taiwan, but when she moved home she found that Hong Kong had little use for sociologists. Undaunted, she sought employment in business management instead. Once employed, she worked her way up through the various departments of an international export/import company.

By 1987 Esther was well established in financial management and her executive position took her all over China. That same year, she met Ming Wong, who was visiting Hong Kong from Canada.

Ming Wong had emigrated from China to Canada with his mother in the 1950s. By the time he met Esther, he had become a Canadian citizen, was living in BC, and was employed as a teacher after graduating from Simon Fraser University. When his Hong Kong trip was over, Esther and Ming parted ways but kept in touch.

Chinese

Chinese Sausage and Shrimp Rice

3 cups (720 mL) hot cooked rice

1½ tbsp (22.5 mL) cooking oil, divided

2 Chinese sausages

3 oz (90 g) shelled small shrimp, fresh or frozen

2 eggs, beaten

½ cup (125 mL) frozen peas, thawed

2 green onions, minced

¼ tsp (1 mL) salt

Grating of pepper

½ tbsp (7.5 mL) oyster sauce

3 tbsp (45 mL) oil

Slice sausage into thin pieces.

Heat ½ tbsp (7.5 mL) oil in a non-stick pan and sauté sausage pieces for 5 minutes. Add shrimp, mix with sausage and sauté for 3 minutes. Set aside.

Add 1 tbsp (15 mL) oil to pan and scramble eggs. Set aside.

Heat 3 tbsp (45 mL) oil in same pan and stir in rice, peas, green onions, salt, pepper and oyster sauce. Mix for 3 minutes.

Add scrambled eggs, sautéed sausage and shrimp; mix well. Serve hot.

Fried Bean Curd with Pork

1½ lbs (750 g) or 2 pieces bean curd (medium tofu)

6 oz (170 g) minced pork

1 tsp (5 mL) each light and dark soy sauce

2 tbsp (30 mL) cooking oil

3 garlic cloves, minced

1½ tbsp (22.5 mL) oyster sauce

Dash of salt

¾ cup (180 mL) water

½ tbsp (7.5 mL) cornstarch dissolved in a little water

2 green onions, diced

Cut bean curd into small pieces.

Marinate the minced pork with the light and dark soy sauce.

Heat oil in a pan and sauté the pork. Add garlic and fry the pork until it breaks apart and is cooked through.

Add the bean curd, oyster sauce, salt and water, and bring to a boil. Add the cornstarch solution and cook a few minutes more.

Remove to serving dish and sprinkle the green onions on top. Serve hot.

Five years passed before Esther made plans to visit Canada and see Ming in 1992. While here, she decided she wanted to stay in Canada with Ming. He agreed. They married that year and Esther started the immigration process.

When Esther arrived in Canada, Ming was living in Williams Lake, BC, but the couple then moved to Bella Coola to start a small business, the Coho Café.

Esther says that living in Bella Coola after Hong Kong was a hard adjustment. "Everything was so different," she says. "The food, so few people, only trees, ocean and mountains, and I knew no one." She knew a bit of English but was not fluent.

A few years after starting the Coho Café, their daughter, Monique, was born. The new parents ran the cafe until 2004 and then closed it and moved back to Williams Lake, where Esther and Ming started the new Coho Restaurant on Second Avenue.

By 2008 they sold the Coho Restaurant, and Ming is now retired. He loves hunting and gardening, and these activities are an important part of his retirement. Esther still has a love of business and might consider working in that field again, but not while Monique is finishing up high school. Ming had a son previous to their marriage who became a dentist. Monique is considering a career in the same field. These days both parents are focused on their children's success.

—Tom Salley

Pat Wong

Pat arrived in Vancouver in 1977 with her husband, Shing Hoi, and their eight-month-old son. Hong Kong had been their home, but Shing Hoi was concerned that the government of China would exert its power and take over Hong Kong. He did not want to live under Communist rule and saw opportunity in Canada, so he moved his young family here. When they immigrated they were initially planning to go to Toront,o where Shing Hoi had lined up work as a machine operator. It so happened that Pat had a sister in Williams Lake and there were job opportunities here too, so they gave it a try and both found employment. Pat explains that the Chinese believe "a bird in the hand is worth two in the bush."

Yong Chow Fried Rice

Any large city in Canada, such as Vancouver or Toronto, has a Chinatown where cooked BBQ pork can be obtained. Some of the larger supermarkets also supply it.

2 tbsp (30 mL) cooking oil

Cooked rice, enough for 3–4 bowls

2 green onions, finely chopped

½ cup (125 mL) cooked peas

1 cup (250 mL) BBQ pork

½ cup (125 mL) cooked shrimp

2 eggs, scrambled

Pinch of salt

1 tsp (5 mL) chicken stock

2 tbsp (30 mL) light soy sauce

Heat a wok and add the cooking oil. Heat the cooked rice in a microwave.

Put the warmed rice in the wok, stir it well and add the remaining ingredients. Mix well until everything is hot.

Sautéed Prawns

The trick to preventing prawns from shrinking is to cook them in the shell.

10–11 tiger prawns, with or without head, tail trimmed, shell on

1 small onion

2 green onions

2 slices of ginger

2 shallots

2 tbsp (30 mL) cooking oil

Seasoning

1 tbsp (15 mL) Worchestershire sauce

1 tbsp (15 mL) light soy sauce

2 tsp (10 mL) sugar

Splash of hot sauce (optional)

A bit of water

Chopped parsley for garnish

Julienne all the vegetables. Heat wok and add oil. Sauté the vegetables.

Add the prawns, the seasoning and a bit of water. Cook until the prawns turn colour. Garnish with parsley.

Shing Hoi found work at a sawmill and saw the chance to move up. He eventually became a lumber grader with an AAA ticket. Pat started working in the restaurant trade, so they had two birds in the hand and that sealed the deal for staying in Williams Lake.

Pat began working as a waitress at the Homesteader Restaurant and was later hired and trained as a cook at the Overlander Restaurant. After eleven years working at the Overlander, Pat set out on her own and purchased Gringo's Restaurant. She successfully operated Gringo's for seventeen years before selling the business and retiring. It is now known as Karen's Place.

Pat says she doesn't want to cook for others anymore but loves to cook for herself at home. She is now travelling, sightseeing and visiting friends around the country as she relaxes into her retirement.

She shares her favourite recipes.

—Tom Salley

Notes

Sweet and Sour Pork

1 lb (500 g) pork tenderloin (or pork butt), cut into 1-inch (2.5-cm) pieces

Marinade

1 tbsp (15 mL) light soy sauce

A few drops of sesame seed oil

1 tsp (5 mL) garlic powder

1 tsp (5 mL) oyster sauce

½ tsp (2.5 mL) salt

1 tsp (5 mL) sugar

Sauce

¼ cup (60 mL) ketchup

2 tsp (10 mL) rice wine

¼ cup (60 mL) vinegar

3 tbsp (45 mL) sugar

¼ tsp (1 mL) salt

3 tbsp (45 mL) cornstarch

⅔ cup (160 mL) water

Egg wash

2 beaten eggs

½ cup (125 mL) milk

Flour to coat pork

Vegetables for garnish

1 green pepper, chopped into 1-inch (2.5 -cm) pieces

1 red pepper, chopped into 1-inch (2.5-cm) pieces

1 small can of pineapple chunks

1 small onion, chopped

Combine marinade ingredients and marinate pork for 20 minutes, then drain.

While pork is marinating, make sauce. Put all sauce ingredients, except cornstarch and water, in a pot over medium heat. Mix well. When sugar has dissolved, mix cornstarch with water and add to pot. When sauce bubbles and thickens, remove from heat and set aside.

Coat pork pieces with egg wash, then roll them in flour until well coated. Fry these in a wok with a small amount of oil until almost done. Add garnish vegetables and cook another few minutes, then add the sauce, heat through and serve.

Coarse rice for food, water to drink, and the bended arm for a pillow — happiness may be enjoyed even in these.

—Confucius

Anne Burrill

Anne was born and raised in the Cariboo Chilcotin. Her parents immigrated to Canada from the United States after working in the Peace Corps in Malaysia and settled in Kleena Kleene. They instilled the value of participation in communities and cultures, and always talked of adopting. So it wasn't odd, when Anne and Glen tied the knot and began to plan for a family, that they decided to explore international adoption. Eventually they adopted two children as infants from Korea—Amelia, now nine years old, and Finn, now three.

Amelia and Finn, though very young when they left Korea, seem to have brought some of their country's cultural prefer-

Above: Finn, Amelia, and Anne enjoying a cool afternoon walk.

Opposite: Amelia and Finn.

Pibimbap
(Rice with vegetables and meat)

12 oz (350 g) lean beef, sliced very thin

2 cups (475 mL) fresh sliced mushrooms

(Use a combination of button mushrooms with shiitake and/or oyster mushrooms.)

5 tbsp (75 mL) oil

2 cups (475 mL) zucchini, sliced ¼ inch (8 mm) thick

2 cups (475 mL) bean sprouts

1 lb (500 g) spinach, large stems removed

2 red or yellow peppers, sliced thinly

1 fresh hot pepper (e.g., jalapeño) (optional)

2 eggs

2 cups (475 mL) rice

Toasted kelp, crumbled for garnish (optional)

Toasted sesame seeds, for garnish (optional)

Seasoning for Beef and Mushrooms

4 tbsp (60 mL) soy sauce

2 tbsp (30 mL) rice wine or vermouth

2 tbsp (30 mL) sugar

3 green onions, white and pale green part only, finely chopped

2 garlic cloves, crushed or finely chopped

2 tbsp (30 mL) toasted sesame seeds

2 tbsp (30 mL) sesame oil

Pinch of salt and freshly ground black pepper

Seasoning for Sprouts and Spinach

1 tbsp (15 mL) soy sauce

3 green onions, sliced into thin rings

3 garlic cloves, crushed or finely chopped

3 tbsp (45 mL) sesame oil

3 tbsp (45 mL) toasted sesame seeds

Pinch of salt and fresh ground pepper

Turn oven to low heat to keep each item warm as you cook.

Cook rice according to directions; cover and keep warm.

Clean spinach thoroughly and blanch for 10 seconds in a pot of boiling water. Immediately rinse under ice-cold water and drain well, squeezing gently to remove all the water. Transfer to bowl and mix with half the seasoning mix. Keep warm.

Toss bean sprouts lightly with remaining seasoning. The sprouts are traditionally cooked by steaming for 3 minutes in a covered pot and then cooling before adding seasoning.

Place beef and mushrooms in separate bowls and pour half of their seasoning over each of them, tossing lightly to coat.

ences to the Cariboo. Anne chuckles that Koreans seem to love seafood at any time for any meal. For example, her kids wake up looking for cold udon soup left over from the night before. This did not seem so unusual until Anne explained that the udon soup is filled with a variety of sea creatures from fish to octopus. Their favourite snack is roasted seaweed. It has been an education and a family cuisine adjustment, to say the least.

When Anne reflects on her children's acceptance in Williams Lake, she says it has all been positive. "The Cariboo seems so

open and welcoming to immigrants." Additionally, Anne and Glen have worked hard to bring bits of the Korean culture back to the Cariboo so that their children can gain a healthy sense of their dual cultural identity. They celebrate Korean holidays such as Lunar New Year and Chuseok (Korean Thanksgiving/Harvest Festival) as a way to share the rich Korean culture with their children, family and friends. Both parents are excited about watching these two lovely children grow up and blend their cultural backgrounds.

Anne shares some of the favourite recipes that she and Glen discovered on their many trips to Korea in the adoption process.

"These are traditional Korean recipes that I have adapted to suit locally available ingredients and cooking approaches," Anne says. "My experience of Korean food is that it is made with fresh ingredients and served hot. Korean food is very healthy and spicy and includes a large portion of fresh vegetables. Enjoy!"

—Tom Salley

Heat 1 tbsp (15 mL) oil in a large heavy skillet until quite hot. Add half the beef and sauté quickly until browned and cooked just through. Remove to a clean bowl and repeat with remaining beef. Keep warm.

Without cleaning the skillet, add 2 tbsp (30 mL) oil and sauté mushrooms on medium heat until wilted and moist, then increase heat for another minute or so until mushrooms absorb all the liquid. Transfer to bowl. Keep warm.

Sauté zucchini and pepper (and optional hot pepper) separately in 1 tbsp (15 mL) oil each and transfer to separate bowls. Keep warm.

Beat eggs together lightly. Pour just enough into a non-stick pan to cover bottom of pan. Cook on medium until nearly dry, flip and cook 15 seconds, then transfer to cutting board. Repeat to use up egg mixture. Slice eggs into thin strips and transfer to bowl.

This is traditionally served in large hot stone bowls with a fresh egg cracked on top, but you can serve it in large soup or pasta bowls or even on plates, using the egg strips as garnish. Alternatively, place all the separate bowls of ingredients on the table and let everyone put their own dish together. Place a scoop of rice in the centre of individual serving bowls and pass everything around. A little hot chili sauce and some sesame oil add some spice. Chopsticks can be an additional challenge!

Hwach'ae

(Korean fruit soup)

Soup base

½ cup (125 mL) honey

1 oz (28 g) ginger, peeled and grated

2 tbsp (30 mL) fresh lemon juice

3 cups (720 mL) grapefruit juice

2 tbsp (30 mL) rice wine or vermouth (optional)

Fruit

1 apple, peeled and diced

1 Asian pear, peeled and diced (or use regular firm pears)

15 seedless grapes

1 peach, peeled and diced

1 cup (250 mL) diced watermelon

1 cup (250 mL) strawberries, halved or quartered

1 orange, sectioned

Mix soup base with the fruit, cover and refrigerate several hours or overnight.

Garnish

1 tbsp (15 mL) pine nuts

1 tsp (5 mL) cinnamon

6 sprigs mint leaves

The true secret to culinary success is starting with fresh ingredients. The Cariboo is blessed with an abundance of market gardens and local farmers.

Yuriko Marshall

Yuriko Marshall and her husband, Brian, met in Japan where they were both attending Josai International University in Togane, Japan. Yuriko was studying international communications, and Brian was an exchange student from Camosun College in Victoria, BC.

When Brian was organizing his stay in Japan, he sought a home-stay for lodging with a Japanese family, and Yuriko's family sponsored Brian for his home-stay. They

Garlic Teriyaki Chicken

2 chicken breasts

Flour to coat the chicken

Vegetable oil for cooking

Cut light scores in both sides of the chicken breasts and dust with flour. Heat some vegetable oil in a frying pan. Fry the chicken on medium heat for 7 to 10 minutes per side. Do not cover. Remove from frying pan and set aside.

Teriyaki sauce

1 tbsp plus 1 tsp (20 mL) honey

1 tbsp (15 mL) brown sugar

2 tbsp (30 mL) soy sauce

3 tbsp (45 mL) boiled water

Dissolve honey and brown sugar in boiled water, add soy sauce and set aside.

Garnish

Sesame oil

2 large garlic cloves, sliced

½ medium onion, sliced

1 cup (250 mL) small white mushrooms, sliced

2 tbsp (30 mL) sake or white wine

In the same frying pan used for the chicken, heat some sesame oil and fry the garlic, onion and mushrooms on medium-low heat until tender. Add sake or white wine to deglaze.

Reduce to low heat, spread the garnish in the pan and lay the fried chicken on top. Pour the teriyaki sauce evenly over the chicken and simmer for 2 minutes.

To serve, place the chicken on a plate, cover with garnish and pour the sauce over it.

became close friends at that time.

While Brian continued with his studies in Japan, Yuriko pursued further education by becoming an exchange student at Camosun College in Canada. After each returned to their respective countries with school courses completed, they stayed in touch. One thing led to another and they ended up getting married. Yuriko returned to BC in 2002 and received immigrant status in 2003.

Right: Yuriko, Brian and their three boys, Liam (L), Julian (with Brian) and Sean (R).

Yuriko has a wide and varied background in her studies and career experiences. After marrying and moving to Canada she found that she had no time to pursue a career because she and Brian decided to start their family. They are now the proud parents of three sons, Sean, Liam and Julian. Yuriko is currently focused on homemaking and raising the young boys while Brian provides for the financial needs of the family in addition to his familial duties.

When asked about the contrasts between Japanese and Canadian cultures, Yuriko says she sees much fewer age and gender barriers in Canada than she was used to in Japan.

Yuriko's family ran a small inn in Kujuku-ri, Japan, which catered mostly to Japanese guests. Traditional Japanese cuisine was served, and Yuriko, her sister and her mother were the chefs. One can only assume that Brian, while on home-stay at the inn, developed not only a caring relationship with Yuriko but also a fondness for her cooking. She shares some of her favourite traditional Japanese recipes with us: Garlic Teriyaki Chicken; Kinoko Takikomi Gohan (mushroom Japanese pilaf); and Wafu Dressing (creamy soy sauce salad dressing).

—Tom Salley

Kinoko Takikomi Gohan
(Japanese mushroom pilaf)

Makes 4 servings

3 oz (85 g) white mushrooms, thinly sliced

3 oz (85 g) shiitake mushrooms, thinly sliced

2 tsp (10 mL) brown sugar

2½ cups (600 mL) water

2 tbsp (30 mL) soy sauce

1 tbsp (15 mL) sesame oil

3 cups (720 mL) sushi rice (such as Kokuho Rose)

Chopped green onion

Toasted sesame seeds

Rinse and drain the rice in a colander for 30 minutes.

In a saucepan, dissolve the brown sugar in water on medium heat, add mushrooms and cook until tender. Remove from heat and add soy sauce. Set aside and cool to room temperature.

Place rice in a rice cooker and add the cooked mushrooms with soy sauce and sesame oil. Start the rice cooker. When rice is done, mix lightly with a rice spatula. Serve in a bowl and sprinkle green onion and sesame seeds on top.

Wafu Dressing
(Creamy soy sauce salad dressing)

2 tsp (10 mL) white vinegar

1 tsp (5 mL) lemon juice

3 tsp (15 mL) soy sauce

2 tsp (10 mL) olive oil

½ tsp (2.5 mL) sesame oil

½ tsp (2.5 mL) honey

1 tbsp (15 mL) mayonnaise

Grated ginger, chopped onion (optional)

Beat all the ingredients together. Add grated ginger or chopped onion (if using). Use it to dress your favourite vegetables or mix it in soft, drained tofu.

Yuriko and Brian cutting their wedding cake.

Manola Khounviseth

The Vietnam War involved not only Vietnam, the United States and China, but also Laos and Cambodia. Manola was only a child in Laos when her family got caught up in the Sino-Vietnam conflict, where Laos was used as a staging centre for the Chinese and Viet Cong troops. Her family decided to escape in 1979. To do this, her father sold all they owned—including their home—to get the funds to hire mercenary soldiers to lead them out of the country to Thailand, where there were refugee camps. The first attempt was unsuccessful and harrowing. The second escape was a success. The family lived in the refugee camp in Thailand for eighteen months while they applied to immigrate to countries of democracy. Canada accepted them as refugees.

Manola and her family landed in Prince George in 1980, sponsored by the Canadian government as refugees for the first year. Two Canadian families were tasked with assisting the Laotians to integrate into Canadian culture. Manola is still grateful to the Loland and Coast families for all the help they provided. She says these folks were largely responsible for her family's successful integration into Canadian culture. The Lolands and Coasts provided friendship, support, information, food, clothing and help in any form it was needed. Manola attended school in Prince George and went on to Brandon

Lapseen
(Laotian beef salad)

1 lb (454 g) beef tenderloin

1 tsp (5 mL) each salt and pepper

1½ tbsp (22.5 mL) fish sauce

¼ medium-sized red onion, thinly sliced

Juice of 2 limes

8 oz (225 g) bean sprouts, washed and drained

Handful of cilantro, roughly chopped

3 green onions, finely chopped

Marinate the beef with salt and pepper for 1 hour. Barbecue the beef until medium rare (do not overcook). Let the meat cool to room temperature and then slice into very thin strips and put in a medium-sized mixing bowl.

Add fish sauce, red onions, lime juice and mix well.

Add bean sprouts, cilantro, green onions and lightly mix.

Serve with sticky rice and a tray of fresh vegetables, such as cucumber, celery, radish and lettuce.

Numchev

(Papaya salad)

1 small green papaya, shredded into small pieces

1–5 fresh red chilies

¼ tsp (1 mL) salt

1–2 garlic cloves

Handful of garlic leaves, chopped into ½-inch (1.25-cm) pieces

1 tsp (5 mL) shrimp paste (optional)

2 tsp (10 mL) white sugar

1 tsp (5 mL) fish sauce

Juice of 2 limes

Half a tomato, cut into chunks

Grind red chilies, salt, garlic, garlic leaves, shrimp paste and sugar into a fine paste in a mortar and pestle. Add lime juice and fish sauce.

Add papaya and tomato to the paste mixture and mix well in the mortar with the pestle. Serve immediately with sticky rice and roast chicken. Do not freeze.

University and eventually to UBC, where she graduated as a pharmacist. Manola married Marco in 1992, and when he was offered a job with the BC Forest Service they moved to Williams Lake. Manola found work at Kornac and Hamm Pharmacy, and in 1996 they had their first child.

When Manola speaks about her love for Canada, she identifies civil rights, freedoms and medical care as the great accomplishments of this country.

Manola shares three traditional Laotian recipes with us.

—Tom Salley

Notes

Laotian Green Leafy Salad

3 hard-boiled eggs

1 chicken breast, cooked and finely chopped

Fried garlic oil (¼ cup/60 mL olive oil and five cloves minced garlic, sautéed)

1 tbsp (15 mL) white sugar

Juice of 2 limes

½ tbsp (7.5 mL) fish sauce

1 head leafy green lettuce, washed, drained and shredded

½ medium-sized English cucumber, cut in half lengthwise and thinly sliced

1 medium-sized ripe tomato, thinly sliced

Handful of chopped cilantro

Shell the boiled eggs and separate the white from the yolk. Set the yolks aside. Slice the egg whites into thin pieces and set aside.

Put chopped chicken, fried garlic oil, sugar, lime juice and fish sauce in a medium-sized-bowl. Mix thoroughly and set aside.

Put the shredded lettuce into a serving bowl and add sliced cucumber, tomato, cilantro and egg whites. Mix well. Add the chicken mixture and stir together.

Just before serving add egg yolk to the salad and mix well. Serve immediately.

Khaeng Kheaw Whan

(Thai green curry)

Makes 2 to 3 servings. Ready in 25 minutes.

1 lb (500 g) chicken, mix of white and dark meat, cut into bite-sized pieces

1 cup (250 mL) coconut milk (divided)

1–2 tbsp (15–30 ml) green curry paste

6–7 quartered eggplants

1 cup (250 mL) water

¼ cup (60 mL) pea eggplants, picked from stem and washed

2 tbsp (30 mL) fish sauce

1 tbsp (15 mL) sugar

1 red sweet chili pepper, thinly sliced length-wise

4–5 kaffir lime leaves

3 sprigs Thai basil

Wash and prepare kaffir lime leaves by ripping the centre stems from the leaves; wash the Thai basil and set both aside.

In a large pot over medium heat pour in half the coconut milk and all the curry paste. Mix well. Stir constantly to keep it from burning. Lower the heat if it splatters too much. Keep stirring until you see a greenish oil form. These are the spices mixing with the coconut oil.

Nirach Suapa

Nick, as he is called at Thompson Rivers University (TRU), fits a common profile of many immigrants today. He is extremely well educated with a Ph.D. and two master's degrees. In fact, it was his pursuit of

Green curry can be hot. Start with less until you find the spice level you like.

Green curry should not be too sweet; it should have just a hint of sweetness.

If your curry paste is old or not quite green, add a few ground fresh pepper leaves. If fresh pepper leaves are not available, use a mild leafy green instead. This will give you a beautiful fresh green without the heat of a chili pepper.

Add the chicken to the curry mix. Stir to coat the chicken in sauce for 2 to 3 minutes. Add the larger eggplants (not the pea eggplants) and stir. Add the rest of the coconut milk and 1 cup water. Let simmer for 10 minutes or until chicken is fully cooked. Add the pea eggplants, the fish sauce and sugar. Mix well. Add the sliced chili pepper and the kaffir lime leaves. Let simmer again. When ready to serve, add the Thai basil. Stir in the basil and immediately take the pot off the heat. Pour into bowls.

www.thaitable.com

I prefer a mixture of white and dark chicken meat to get the correct flavour for the curry.

—*Nick*

higher education that brought him from Thailand to Canada to earn his doctorate. He ended up at the University of Regina in the graduate program for education, and received his Ph.D. in 2011.

Nick landed the position of facilitator of TRU's Open Learning Program at the Aboriginal Learning Centre—"The Gathering Place"—on the Williams Lake Campus. He moved to Williams Lake with his wife, Tip, four-year-old daughter, Neen, and one-year-old son, Bhoopa.

When asked what makes Canada an appealing place to live, Nick says good infrastructure, not much crime, respect for law, and unified standards for policies, goods and services. He wants to raise and educate his family here.

Nick does most of the cooking in his family. In Thailand people like to drink and enjoy food during their festivities. Nick realized he needed to learn to cook in order to entertain family and friends. He says his mom

Left: Nick with his wife, Tip (back right), their daughter, Neen (left) and son, Bhoopa (right).

Pad Thai

Pad Thai is the traditional street food of Thailand. It can also be a vegetarian dish by substituting soy sauce for fish sauce and omitting the shrimp.

Makes 2–3 servings. Ready in 40 minutes.

½ package Thai rice noodles

⅓ cup (80 mL) extra-firm tofu, julienned into inch-long (2.5-cm) matchsticks

1 ⅓ cup (325 mL) bean sprouts (optional)

1 minced shallot

3 garlic cloves, minced

2 tbsp (30 mL) vegetable oil

2 tbsp (30 mL) peanuts (optional)

1 tbsp (15 mL) preserved turnip

2 tbsp (30 mL) tamarind paste, or white vinegar

2 tbsp (30 mL) sugar

4 tsp (20 mL) fish sauce

½ tsp (2.5 mL) ground dried chili pepper

1 egg

¼ to ½ lb (110–225 g) shrimp

Ground white pepper to taste

1½ cup (350 mL) Chinese chives, cut into 1-inch (2.5-cm) pieces (optional)

½ lime

½ banana flower (optional)

helped him to refine his cooking skills. It takes skill to put together the blend of sweet, sour, salty and spicy herbs in just the right combination that characterizes good Thai food.

The recipes that Nick is sharing: Khaeng Kheaw Whan (green curry), Pad Thai (noodle stir-fry), and Tom Yum Goong (shrimp in spicy soup) have been adapted from recipes available at www.thaitable. com and have been reprinted with the permission of Thai Table. Nick says these recipes are authentic and use the same methods and ingredients as his mom learned in Thailand.

—Tom Salley

Soak the noodles in lukewarm water until noodles are flexible but not soft. (See hint below.)

Rinse the bean sprouts and reserve half to serve fresh. Mince shallot and garlic together.

Over high heat, add oil to wok or large pot. Fry the peanuts until roasted, remove from wok and set aside.

Add shallot, garlic, preserved turnip and tofu to wok and stir until they start to brown. Drain noodles and add to wok, stirring quickly. Add tamarind, sugar, fish sauce and chili pepper. Mix well. If mixture is too juicy, turn up heat.

Push mixture to one side of the wok and add egg. Scramble the egg until almost cooked and then fold in with noodles. Noodles should now be soft and chewy. If not, add a bit of water.

When the noodles are done, add shrimp and stir. Sprinkle with white pepper. Add half the bean sprouts and 1 cup (250 mL) chives, saving the rest for garnish. Stir.

Pour onto serving plate. Sprinkle with peanuts and ground pepper. Put raw chives and fresh bean sprouts on top. Serve hot with banana flower slice and a wedge of lime on the side. More spices can be added at the table for individual tastes.

Hints: Noodles should be somewhat flexible and solid, not completely expanded and soft. When in doubt, under-soak. You can always add more water later.

If you use banana flower, cut lengthwise like orange sections and cover cuts with lime juice to keep them from turning dark.

Tofu can be fried ahead of time until golden brown, or with other ingredients as listed in the method.

www.thaitable.com

Tom Yum Goong

This is Nirach's favourite recipe for making Tom Yum Goong. It's simple and fast.

Makes 2 servings. Ready in 20 minutes.

1 cup (250 mL) shrimp

4 cups (1 L) water

1 lemongrass stalk

2 tbsp (30 mL) fish sauce

Juice of 2 limes

3 chili peppers, crushed

3 kaffir lime leaves

5 mushrooms, cleaned and sliced in half

5 sprigs cilantro

1 tbsp (15 mL) Nam Prig Pow (optional)

Peel and de-vein the shrimp and set aside.

Boil water in a 2-quart (2 L) pot. Cut the lemongrass into pieces 5 to 6 inches (12 to 15 cm) long. Use the back of a knife to pound the lemongrass so it will bruise and release

Nam Prig Pow is a dark brown chili paste from Thailand. The core ingredients are shallots, garlic, shrimp paste, dry chili pepper, salt and sugar. Frequently tamarind paste and dried shrimp are included.

adapted from www.thaitable.com

its flavour. Tie the lemongrass into a knot, drop it into boiling water and boil for 5 minutes.

Divide the fish sauce and the lime juice between two serving bowls. Crush the chili peppers and add to the bowls.

Remove the stems of the kaffir lime leaves and add the leafy part to the pot of water. Add the mushrooms and bring to a boil. Add the shrimp and turn off the heat. The shrimp will cook in the boiled water.

Add the shrimp and liquid from the pot to the prepared serving bowls. The liquid will become cloudy as it mixes with the lime juice. Add the Nam Prig Pow. Sprinkle with cilantro and serve.

www.thaitable.com

Spicy Squash Mango Soup

2 butternut squash or any type of orange squash

One 1¾-lb (850-g) can of puréed mangos

½ cup (125 mL) fresh grated ginger

½ tsp (2.5 mL) cloves

½ tsp (2.5 mL) cinnamon

2 tsp (10 mL) salt or to taste

Cilantro or parsley, finely chopped

Bake squash and remove skin after cooling.

Using a blender or food processor, combine squash with ginger and enough water to make a creamy consistency, not too thick or too thin.

Add spices to mango in a saucepan and bring to a boil.

Add squash and ginger mixture. Simmer for about half an hour, adding water to the soup if needed.

Sprinkle with freshly chopped cilantro or parsley before serving.

Martin Comtois

Martin Comtois was born in Montreal, where he and his two brothers were raised by their single mom. Martin says his mother turned "alternative, new age, or hippy," as some might call it, and this exposed him to new influences.

Montreal was, and still is, very multicultural, and growing up there, Martin got to sample all the fabulous food that this cosmopolitan city had to offer.

His family really enjoyed eating. Big, elaborate meals were served every Sunday after church at his grandmother's house, mostly featuring traditional French-Canadian cuisine. The European influence was strong too, and his mother always brought back interesting recipes from her trips abroad while working as a travel agent. The recipes came from France, Morocco, Mexico and beyond. "We got to see those countries through their cuisine," Martin says.

For Martin, cooking came early in life. "It sounds weird to say, but my favourite plaything when I was a kid, besides my toy soldiers and my hockey stick, was an Easy-Bake oven."

In the late 1970s Martin travelled to California and joined a Hare Krishna community. His spiritual master used to say the Hare Krishna religion was a kitchen religion. By the time Martin was twenty he was cooking and running the kitchen for a community of sixty in San Diego, sometimes cooking feasts for up to four hundred people. That's where he learned how to cook for the masses. While there, he totally immersed himself in the age-old art of East Indian cuisine.

After his temple days, Martin spent a decade farming in Hawaii where he was introduced to the culinary traditions of the Japanese, Chinese, Thai and Polynesians. In the late 1990s he ended up in Ashcroft, BC, running his own Secret Garden Restaurant. When it burned down, Martin refocused his energies on renovating the Ashcroft Opera House, where he hosted fabulous dinner concerts with great music and delicious food.

Martin moved to Williams Lake in 2010 and still loves to cook for dinner concerts, festivals and community events. He also

Thai Spring Roll

Rice-paper spring roll wrappers are found in the ethnic section of most grocery stores. Amounts of ingredients will vary according to number of servings.

Cabbage, carrots and beets, grated

Bean sprouts

Tofu

Green onions

Coriander leaves

Chop all vegetables (except bean sprouts) and keep them separated.

In a metal bowl big enough to submerge the rice papers, pour boiling water. Dip rice papers in hot water and lay them on a clean working surface, making sure to keep them flat and unfolded.

Fill the centre of each rice paper with assorted grated vegetables, sprouts, tofu or whatever you desire, leaving the edges clean for folding.

Fold bottom edge up about halfway. Fold right and left side to create an envelope. Wetting the last edge, fold the envelope closed, making sure it is tight. It takes some practice to make the rolls consistent and firm.

Arrange on a serving platter and serve with Peanut Sauce (recipe below) or other favourite sauces.

Peanut Sauce

1 lb (500 g) peanut butter

¼ cup (60 mL) freshly grated ginger

2–3 freshly chopped cerona chilies, or more to taste

¾ cup (180 mL) lemon juice

One 12-oz (340-mL) can coconut milk

½ cup (125 mL) Bragg's liquid aminos or tamari

Blend all ingredients in a blender or food processor, adding a little water to obtain proper consistency.

This can also be made as a salad dressing with a bit more water and fewer chilies.

runs an astrology practice and is a writer and painter. On his website, www.mountainmystics.ca, you can access more of Martin's recipes and learn about his work.

Here are a few of Martin's favourite Thai recipes for your dining pleasure.

—Martin Comtois with Tom Salley

Bea Dodd

Bea grew up in Manila in the Philippines. One of eleven children, she started cooking with her mother at seven years old. She recalls having to stand on a small stool to reach the counter. The first thing she learned to cook was a traditional Filipino dish called Adobo. She instantly fell in love with cooking and it has been her passion all her life.

Bea's mother also taught her to do other domestic chores, such as cleaning and ironing with great precision. Bea still enjoys these tasks and thinks of her mother and misses her as she does them.

Pork Adobo

2 lbs (1 kg) pork, cut into 2-inch (5-cm) cubes

1 tbsp (15 mL) soy sauce, or to taste

1 garlic clove, minced or finely chopped

½ tbsp (7.5 mL) peppercorns

½ small onion, chopped

5 bay leaves

⅓ cup (80 mL) vinegar, or juice of one lemon

1 cup (250 mL) water

1–2 tbsp (15–30 mL) vegetable oil

¼ each green, red and orange bell peppers, chopped (optional)

1–2 tbsp (15–30 mL) fresh chopped parsley

Marinate pork in soy sauce, garlic and peppercorns in the fridge for at least 1 to 2 hours or overnight.

Sauté onion in oil. Add the marinated pork and bay leaves. Reserve the marinade. If desired, sauté a bit of garlic before adding the onion. Continue sautéing until liquid has evaporated and starts to render fat. Don't allow the pork to dry out.

Add the marinade and water. Cover and simmer over medium-low heat until pork is tender.

Add the peppers, if using. Add vinegar or

lemon juice and simmer until sauce is reduced. Just before serving add the chopped parsley.

Serve hot on top of cooked rice.

Hint: Cooking the pork without vinegar or lemon at the beginning of the cooking procedure tenderizes the pork faster. Only add the vinegar or lemon *after* the pork is tender.

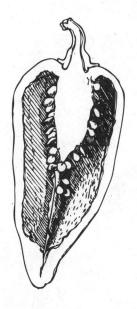

Opposite page: Bea Dodd with her mother.

While working in her kitchen in Manila, Bea dreamt of travelling to different places in the world. She lived in an all-women dormitory doing her post-secondary bachelor of science in nursing. After she graduated, Bea began to fulfill her dreams of travel. She lived in England for fourteen years, a short distance from London, and her son, Kris, was born there. She has travelled to Europe many times and loves the hustle and bustle of the large cities. "I am a city girl," she says. Unexpectedly, Bea's husband passed away and a new life chapter began to unfold.

She was introduced to George Dodd, who became her second husband, and has been living in Williams Lake for the past twelve years. Bea and Kris had to make a huge transition, from city to country, leaving friends and family. Bea was totally amazed by the eight-hour drive to Williams Lake. For the first time in her life she heard the wind blowing and the birds singing and was pleasantly surprised by the fresh air. At first she says it was a bit lonely adjusting to a new country, but she doesn't regret a thing.

Kris has adjusted too, and is awaiting his first child. Bea will soon be a grandmother.

—Marilyn Livingston

Tastes of Australia, South Africa and Fiji

Sonya Wells

It has been only a year since Sonya Wells and her family left the balmy climate of Australia to test out the four seasons of the Cariboo. However, if you looked at the places they've been in the region and the activities they have been involved with, you'd swear they have been here ten years. When Sonya's Canadian friends mention a pretty lake in the Chilcotin or a community festival, rest assured, they have already been there.

They have tried every winter sport imaginable and, much to Sonya's chagrin, her husband, Patrick, has fallen in love with the simple pleasures of ice fishing. His enthusiasm for the sport propels the family out of bed and into the beautiful Cariboo winter many a weekend morning. A keen observer might notice Sonya huddled in the car with the heat on long before Patrick is ready to call it a day. Their children, Flynn, Liam and Ayla, had never seen

Anzac Biscuits

Makes 50 biscuits

1 cup (250 mL) rolled oats

1 cup (250 mL) sifted flour

1 cup (250 mL) sugar

¾ cup (180 mL) dessicated coconut

¾ cup (180 mL) butter

2 tbsp (30 mL) golden syrup

2 tbsp (30 mL) boiling water

1½ tsp (7.5 mL) baking soda

Preheat oven to 300°F (150°C).

Combine rolled oats, flour, sugar and coconut in a large bowl.

Melt butter and syrup in a small saucepan. Mix boiling water and baking soda together. Blend into butter mixture. Pour over dry ingredients and mix well.

Drop biscuit dough by the teaspoonful onto lightly greased cookie sheets. Allow room for spreading.

Bake in preheated oven for 15 to 20 minutes. Loosen from cookie sheet while still warm and cool for 5 minutes. Store in an airtight container.

Opposite page: Sonya Wells ice fishing with her family.

Lamb Rack with Feta and Oregano Crust

3 lamb racks, excess fat removed

2 oz (57 g) crumbled feta cheese

1 cup (250 mL) bread crumbs from day-old bread

¼ cup (60 mL) fresh chopped oregano

2 large garlic cloves, crushed

3 tbsp (45 mL) Dijon mustard

olive oil

2 cups (500 mL) beef stock

1½ cups (375 mL) dry red wine

1½ cups (375 mL) light cream

Preheat oven to 400°F (205°C).

Put feta, bread crumbs, oregano and garlic in a small bowl. Mix until combined.

Smear 1 tbsp of mustard onto each of the lamb racks. Then press breadcrumb mixture firmly onto mustard to coat the lamb. Place in a roasting pan and drizzle a little olive oil over the meat. Cook in preheated oven for 25 minutes for medium well-done or until cooked to your liking.

Place stock and red wine in large frying pan and bring to a boil, reduce heat and simmer until liquid is reduced by half. Add the cream and simmer for 5 to 10 minutes or until sauce is thickened.

Serve lamb with sauce, mashed potatoes and steamed vegetables.

snow before but, despite the cold, they now love all things winter.

The move to Williams Lake was not a spur-of-the-moment decision. Sonya recalls that she and Patrick had always talked about coming to Canada. Patrick's great-aunt lives in Vancouver and he had visited when he was fifteen years old. So when Orica, the mining explosives company for whom Patrick works, posted a position for Williams Lake, they were quick to jump at the chance. Sonya resigned from her job as a registered nurse on a general hospital ward and has been enjoying the time that she is able to spend with their children. She also has a passion for photography. "I like to get out, take some photos, and enjoy nature," she explains. In fact, since coming to Canada, she has taken over ten thousand photos.

Australia has quite a varied cuisine. There is the staple English food, a reminder of the country's early days as a convict colony;

Greek influences in the south; Italian cuisine from the cane field workers in the north; and Asian-inspired cuisine around Darwin. Lamb is a common dish and one that many people associate with Australia, but kangaroo, crocodile and emu are also popular delicacies. Unique to that area of the world is the ANZAC biscuit, so named for its use by the Australia and New Zealand Army Corps (ANZAC) in the First World War. It is a sweet biscuit that wives would send to the soldiers abroad because of its ability to travel well. Sonya says that it is one of those foods for which everyone has their own family recipe, each slightly different than the others.

Sonya is not certain how long her family will be in the Cariboo, but for now they are making the most of their Canadian adventure.

— Margaret-Anne Enders

Golden Syrup Dumplings

Best served on vanilla ice cream.

1¾ cups (225 g) self-rising flour

¼ cup (60 mL) chilled butter

½ cup (125 mL) light cream

1 tbsp (15 mL) golden syrup

1 egg, at room temperature

Sift the flour into a large bowl. Use your fingertips to rub in the butter until the mixture resembles fine bread crumbs. Make a well in the centre. Combine the cream, syrup and egg. Add to the dry ingredients and use a wooden spoon to mix until well combined.

Sauce

2 cups (500 mL) water

½ cup (125 mL) golden syrup

½ cup (125 mL) firmly packed brown sugar

⅜ cup (75 mL) butter

Place the water, syrup, sugar and butter in a large saucepan. Stir over medium heat until the sugar dissolves. Increase the heat to high and bring to a boil, then reduce heat to medium. Add heaped teaspoons of the dough into the sauce. Simmer, covered for 15 to 20 minutes or until a toothpick comes out clean.

Divide the dumplings into serving bowls with the sauce and serve immediately with vanilla ice cream.

Palusami

The traditional way to cook Palusami is in an underground earthern oven, known as a Lovo. This dish is nutritious, filling and easy to make, and it's great either hot or cold.

1–2 dozen medium-sized taro leaves (or spinach/Swiss chard leaves)

1 medium-sized can of corned beef, or substitute

1 small can of coconut milk

Several roughly sliced tomatoes

1–2 onions, sliced into rings

Garlic cloves, crushed

Pinch of dried sage and thyme

Preheat oven to 350°F (175°C).

Remove the thickest parts of the taro stalks and put them in a bowl of hot water while you prepare the main ingredients.

Mix the corned beef with some of the coconut milk to obtain a mix that holds together. Add the crushed garlic and herbs.

Line a medium-sized baking dish with enough tinfoil to fold the top over and seal it. Arrange the taro leaves along the bottom and sides of the dish, overlapping them so that there are no gaps.

Put half the corned beef mixture in, and top with a layer of tomato slices and onion rings.

Paul Lomavatu

Paul Lomavatu grew up in the island nation of Fiji. At age twenty-seven, he followed a sense of God's call to come to Canada to pursue ministry. While it was a huge change for him, it gave him the space and opportunities he had been yearning for. He describes growing up in Fiji as similar to being a frog in a pond. When he put his head up out of the water, he saw a whole new world that he longed to encounter.

Paul attended the Youth With A Mission (YWAM) discipleship training program in Falkland, BC, where he met his future wife, Clarice. They were married and started their family while Paul completed a degree in intercultural studies at Prairie Bible Institute. In 1995, Paul and Clarice moved to Williams Lake. Here they have raised their four children, Robert, Avikali, Ana and Naomi. Paul has been the pastor of Cariboo Community Church for the past thirteen years. He notes that he has now been in Canada longer than he had lived in Fiji and has noticed that he now thinks, speaks and acts in ways that are more western.

While Paul has immersed himself in the western culture, he remains true to one of the core values of Fijian culture: relationship. Partly due to the geographical characteristics of being an island nation, the Fijian people have close-knit families. Paul explains that you *are* your "brother's keeper," and the family clan looks after you in return. Family plots of land are passed down through the generations, and the sense of "home" remains constant and connected to the land. Here in Canada, where people are more transient, Paul's sense of home has taken on a different meaning. The physical connection to land, clan and burial plots has given way to "the place where the kids always come to." While the house or the community may change for the Lomavatus, the strong relationships within their family are the foundation of their home.

Paul's innate desire for relationship extends beyond his family. "Being with people is what gives me life," he affirms. He lives out his faith through his care for his congregation and the people in the wider community. As in many places, food is a big part of hospitality in the Fijian culture. This sense of hospitality has been experienced in Williams Lake through Paul's

Add the rest of the beef, and finish with the last of the tomatoes and onions.

Pour a little coconut milk over the mixture, and bend the taro leaves over the top, securing with toothpicks. Cover with the foil, and bake for 30 minutes.

Traditional Fijian Miti

Miti originated in Fiji and is a delicious, rich coconut sauce or relish eaten with prepared fish. The main ingredient in Miti is "lolo," or coconut cream. Lolo can be made from desiccated coconut (see recipe below) or canned coconut milk/cream.

Miti

1½ cups (350 mL) lolo (thick coconut cream/coconut milk)

Juice of 2 lemons

¼ tsp (1 mL) sea salt (or to taste)

1 small hot red chili, finely minced (use more if preferred)

1 tomato, finely chopped

1 small red onion, minced

Put all ingredients in a bowl, mix together and let sit for an hour. Serve as a cold relish with prepared fish.

Lolo

1 cup (250 mL) desiccated coconut

½ cup (125 mL) boiling water

Pour the boiling water into a bowl with the desiccated coconut. Let sit for a few hours, then squeeze and wring it through muslin or cheesecloth.

sharing of the traditional Fijian Lovo feast. The Lovo is a cooking pit or earth oven in which the food is cooked on hot stones and covered by earth. Meat, fish and vegetables are all infused with a delicate smoky flavour. It is a taste of Fiji in the Cariboo, where the food is plentiful, the spirits are high, friendships are made and relationships are celebrated.

— Margaret-Anne Enders

Jale Bulamaibau from Fiji, performing at Paul's Lovo.

Cecilia Newman

Cecilia grew up in Capetown, South Africa, in a big rambling house with her parents, grandparents, uncle and six siblings. Her grandfather had a carpentry shop at the back of the house where he made fine carved and inlaid wood furniture for department stores. The neighbourhood where they lived is known as District 6, the designated area for "Cape Coloureds." It has since been razed to the ground, rambling house and all.

For Cecilia and her husband, Leslie, the decision to leave South Africa was a slow and careful process. Cecilia's sister-in-law travelled all over the world as a nanny and had for many years extolled the virtues

Bobotie

This is a traditional Cape dish from South Africa.

2 lbs (1 kg) ground beef (or 1 lb minced lamb combined with 1 lb minced beef)

2 tbsp (30 mL) oil

2 medium-sized onions, chopped

2 slices of bread, crumbled ·

1 medium yellow turnip, grated or finely chopped

1 apple, shredded

1 tbsp (15 mL) curry powder, or according to taste

2 tbsp (30 mL) finely chopped almonds

1 tbsp (15 ml) vinegar or lemon juice

2 tbsp (30 mL) raisins

1 tsp (5 ml) turmeric

1 tsp (5 mL) grated fresh ginger (optional)

2 tsp (10 mL) salt

1 beaten egg

1 cup (250 ml) beef stock

4 whole almonds (or more) for top

2 bay leaves or lemon leaves for top

Fry onion in oil in saucepan until transparent. Turn up heat and brown ground beef. Lower heat, stir in bread crumbs and turnips. Mix well. Add apple and continue cooking. Mix together curry, nuts, vinegar or lemon juice, raisins, turmeric, ginger (if using) and salt, and add to meat mixture. Add beaten egg. Stir in beef stock and simmer for 10 minutes. Transfer to 9x9-inch (23x23-cm) ovenproof dish or metal pan. Place bay leaves and whole almonds in a pattern on top (remove bay leaves before serving). Bake, covered with a sheet of tin foil, in 350°F (175°C) oven for 25 minutes.

Optional: Beat egg and ¼ cup (60 mL) milk together and pour over the meat. Return to oven and bake uncovered until the milk mixture has set, 8 to 15 minutes. Serve with rice.

Hint: Tastes good cold on a sandwich.

Chicken Curry (mild)

8 chicken pieces

4 tbsp oil (60 ml)

2 onions, chopped

1 sweet apple, cored and chopped

¼ cup (60 mL) flour or cornstarch

1 tbsp (15 mL) curry powder

1¼ cup (300 mL) chicken stock

2 tbsp (30 mL) jam or 1 tbsp (15 mL) honey or cranberry sauce

and opportunities of living abroad. Finally, in 1965, the family immigrated to Scotland, where Leslie had secured a teaching position. As their exit permits from South Africa were delayed, Leslie flew north at the last minute and Cecilia followed by boat with all four children. After two years they came to Canada, looking for a home where it didn't rain every day as it did in Scotland.

Once in Canada, the Newmans' destination was Prince George. On the train across the country, some of their new travelling friends warned them not to go to Prince George. "It's frontier country, with people shooting at each other." They were disbelieving and undeterred, but it was

Cecilia Newman with her sisters, mother and grandmother.

quite a shock when they arrived in the city and saw all the pitted windshields. With a laugh, Cecilia recalls thinking, "It's true!" After two years in Prince George, they moved to Chezacut, in the Chilcotin, where Leslie was hired to start up the school. The community was thrilled to have them there and the ranchers gave Cecilia a huge, troublesome pig to look after. She had to feed him when he was asleep to avoid being chased around the pen.

They lived in the one-room teacherage for five months, by which time Cecilia had enough of being a pioneer wife. She moved into Williams Lake with the children and kept the home fires burning until Leslie could join them. This took a few years, as Leslie had to finish his contract in Chezacut, and then upgrade his teaching degree on the coast.

All these years later, Cecilia is still there, a very vibrant woman and active in the community. She ran the Timmus Thrift Shop for many years and is now on the board of the Association for Community Living, her former employer. She also volunteers with hospice and the old age pensioners, and is active in the Anglican Church. Of course she cooks, still serving dishes like Soetkoekies and Bobotie, which were favourites in South Africa.

—Margaret-Anne Enders

1 tbsp lemon juice or vinegar

Salt and pepper

2 tbsp (30 mL) raisins

Heat oil in a large pan and fry chicken until golden brown. Remove to an 8x8-inch (20x20-cm) casserole dish.

Fry onion and apple in remaining oil until transparent. Add to chicken.

In a medium-sized pot mix flour or cornstarch with curry powder. Gradually add the chicken stock and bring to a boil over medium-high heat, stirring constantly. Add the jam or honey, lemon juice or vinegar, salt and pepper and raisins, mix well and pour over chicken. Cover and cook at 350°F (175°C) for 45 minutes.

Serve with potatoes or rice, chopped cucumber and tomato.

Stewed Sweet Potatoes

1 sweet potato (about 1 lb/500 g), sliced

¼ cup (60 mL) brown sugar or honey

1 tbsp (15 mL) butter or margarine

1 stick cinnamon or piece of raw ginger, peeled

1 tbsp (15 mL) water

Layer sliced sweet potato with sugar or honey and butter in saucepan until all potato is used up. Tuck in the cinnamon or ginger, add water and simmer gently on low heat until soft. Serve with custard of your choice.

Can also be tried in a microwave. Omit the water. Use the baked potato setting or heat for about 12 minutes.

Soetkoekies
(Traditional South African cookies)

2 cups (475 mL) flour

1 tsp (5 mL) salt

2 tsp (10 mL) ground cloves

2 tsp (10 mL) cinnamon

1 tsp (5 mL) ginger

1 tsp (5 mL) baking soda

1 cup (250 mL) white sugar

⅔ cup (160 mL) butter

2 beaten eggs

2 tbsp (30 mL) sherry or orange juice

Preheat oven to 350°F (175°C).

Sift together dry ingredients, rub in butter. Add eggs and sherry or orange juice. Knead well. Roll out to ¾- to 1¼-inch (1.5 to 2 cm) thickness. Cut into shapes. Bake for 10 to 15 minutes until lightly brown.

My favourite culinary discovery while in South Africa 15 years ago was rooibos tea. In my mind it has all of the richness of a black tea and all the healthy perks of a herb tea.

—Margaret-Anne Enders

Therisa Peimer

Therisa's story of immigration started when she married a young South African doctor, Jeff Peimer. Not long after tying the knot, they started a family with the arrivals of Dani and Ilan.

The transition period to full democracy had been difficult for South Africa, so when Dr. Peimer was offered an emergency room position with an actual schedule and days off (unheard of in South Africa), Therisa and her family jumped at it. They emigrated from South Africa in August 2011.

Tomato Bredie
(South African stew)

This is a traditional South African dish that was introduced by the "Cape coloured," the slave population that emigrated from Indonesia, Malaysia and Java.

2 large onions, finely chopped

2 tbsp (30 mL) sunflower oil

2 lbs (1 kg) mutton knuckles or stewing mutton

2 lbs (1 kg) ripe tomatoes, skinned and chopped or puréed

4 garlic cloves, minced

1 tsp (5 mL) salt

1 dry red chili, crushed (optional)

2 tbsp (30 mL) tomato paste

4 medium potatoes, quartered

2 tbsp (30 mL) brown sugar or to taste

Braise the onions in oil until brown, about 10 minutes.

Add meat and simmer over medium heat for 30 to 40 minutes, stirring from time to time.

Add tomatoes, garlic, salt, chili and tomato paste and simmer for another 20 minutes.

Add potatoes and cook until tender. Add sugar and cook for another 5 minutes. Serve with rice and vegetables.

Hint: Do not add sugar before the potatoes as it will prolong their cooking time.

Since arriving in Williams Lake, Therisa has immersed herself in the small-town culture they moved halfway around the world to find. She is actively involved in thespian pursuits with the Williams Lake Theatre Club and has been instructing some Italian cooking courses through Elder College. In the future she intends to volunteer for Stampede and take up mountain biking. The family hopes to explore the great outdoors in the Cariboo Chilcotin and become familiar with the cultures, characters and critters that make this wild region home.

The Peimer family is very musical. Between them they play piano, acoustic guitar, electric guitar, bass guitar, drums, and are trained in voice. On that front, we can literally expect to hear more from them in the future.

As a newly arrived immigrant, Therisa says that she has been completely overwhelmed by the friendliness and helpfulness of the people in the Cariboo. "I have never met people so sincere in their intent and actions."

Therisa's family is unique in that it straddles three distinct cultures: South African, Italian and Jewish/Lithuanian. She shares with us a recipe from each of those cultures.

—Tom Salley

Fresh Foods for Fresh Thoughts

1. You are what you eat, so eat best and eat well by eating with conscious intent, creativity and the well-being of your community in mind.

2. Use the freshest food products available for the best-tasting results.

3. Shop locally or close to home when buying ingredients for your recipe. Local products are harvested when ripe and are the freshest, tastiest and most nutritious food available. Locally grown food is also free of cross-border treatment for pests and has not been stored for long periods in coolers.

4. Grow your own food. Any gardener will testify that it doesn't get any fresher than picked from your own garden. Also, gardening is good for your health and budget and for the planet.

5. Explore your food choice options and find out about the food network in your community. Growers' coop-

Brisket in Ginger Ale

One 3-lb (1.5 kg) beef brisket

1 package dry onion soup mix

One 12-oz (340-mL) can ginger ale

1 cup (250 mL) ketchup

3 bay leaves

10 peppercorns

1 onion, sliced

Preheat oven to 350°F (175°C).

Place brisket in a roasting pan. Mix onion soup, ginger ale, ketchup, bay leaves, peppercorns and sliced onion and pour over brisket. Cover and bake for 2 hours.

Remove cover and cook for another hour, basting often with the pan juices. Serve with rice, potatoes or couscous.

Italian

Italian Pork Ribs

This dish is very versatile and can be eaten over pasta, polenta or rice. The ribs can be eaten on or off the bone.

4½ lbs (2 kg) country-style ribs

1–2 tbsp (15–30 mL) olive oil

1 large onion, chopped

2–3 carrots, chopped

3 celery stalks, chopped

8 oz (225 g) bacon, chopped

1 small can tomato paste

2 cups (475 mL) red wine

2 cups (475 mL) beef stock

2–3 tbsp (30–45 mL) chopped Italian parsley

3 bay leaves

1 tbsp (15 mL) thyme

Salt and pepper

Heat olive oil in a large pot over medium-high heat and cook onion, carrots, celery and bacon until bacon is browned and crispy.

Add pork ribs to the pot and fry until browned. Add tomato paste, wine, beef stock, parsley, bay leaves, thyme and salt and pepper and simmer for 2 to 3 hours or until meat is very tender.

eratives, farmers' markets, CSA or box-a-week programs, urban, farm or ranch gate sales, and retailers that stock local foods are your best bet for fresh food.

6. Buying locally grown food supports your neighbours and family farms, builds rural economies, protects genetic diversity and increases regional food security.

7. Organically grown foods reduce greenhouse gas emissions by reducing food-associated transportation costs and/or reducing emissions from oil-based fertilizers. Buying organically grown foods also helps to reduce pesticide and fertilizer runoff into rivers, lakes and streams.

8. In Canada, "organic" labelled products means that the farm the food came from has been regularly inspected by certified inspectors for compliance with National Canadian (organic processing and input) Standards. Non-organic farms in Canada are not regularly inspected or audited for practices.

9. Organic farmers are not allowed to use or grow GMO seeds or food products. Farmers who practise "sustainable" agriculture are more likely to avoid GM products too.

10. A conscientious fresh food shopper's guide: Buy locally grown foods, but if not locally or regionally produced then buy organic; if not organic then from a family farm that practises sustainable agriculture; if not from a family farm then from a local business.

—Tom Salley

Afterword

What started out as a spark from a brainstorming session in Marilyn Livingston's and Tom Salley's office in the spring of 2012 has come to pass.

We envisioned a cultural cookbook to raise awareness of the diversity in our community. It fit perfectly with the mandate of the Multiculturalism Program at the Canadian Mental Health Association Cariboo Chilcotin Branch (CMHA CCB).

In the beginning, we interviewed first-generation immigrants to Canada but soon knew we wanted to portray the larger cultural mosaic that included families of earlier immigrants to the area and local First Nations. In early summer 2012 we asked Margaret-Anne Enders to join us in capturing additional interviews needed for *Spicing Up the Cariboo*.

We all shared similar immensely enjoyable experiences interviewing and learning of the wonderfully diverse backgrounds and beginnings of our fellow citizens of the Cariboo Chilcotin. It was an honour to write a small piece of each participant's story and to learn their family's recipes.

In a project such as this, there are many people to thank. We are grateful to the people who stepped forward for *Spicing Up the Cariboo* and shared with us. We also relied on and are thankful to Sage Birchwater for being our mentor from the conception of the cookbook and Christian Petersen for his expertise in the kitchen and with a pen. Their input was invaluable in bringing the manuscript together. Thanks to Cathie Allen for the delightful painting that graces the cover.

Thank you from all of us to the supportive leadership at CMHA CCB: Bettina Schoen, our program manager who sublimely led the project, and Executive Director Trevor Barnes and the CMHA CCB board members, who encourage and trust the Multiculturalism Program staff with our array of projects and events. We gratefully acknowledge the financial assistance of the Province of British

Columbia and the support of the Cariboo Regional District and City of Williams Lake through the Central Cariboo Arts and Culture Society.

Finally, we are indebted to Vici Johnstone at Caitlin Press, for deciding the project had merit and for leading us through the publishing process, and Patricia Wolfe, whose patience and attention to detail in the editing process transformed our diverse pieces into a cohesive whole.

—Margaret-Anne, Marilyn and Tom

Index of Recipes

At the age of seventeen, **Margaret-Anne Enders** headed off from her small hometown in Alberta to study at Atlantic College in Wales, which is part of the United World College movement. Her experiences there solidified her interest in cross-cultural learning, food, friendships, and travelling. She now lives in Williams Lake, BC, with her husband and two sons. Margaret-Anne is committed to nourishing her family with homemade, organic and local foods.

Ten years ago **Marilyn Livingston**, with her husband and three children, moved to an off-grid wilderness ranch at Taltla Lake. One of the many benefits of the ranch life is having the time to cook, and Marilyn loves to cook. Marilyn is the Multicultural Program Coordinator for the Canadian Mental Health Association Cariboo Chilcotin Branch in Williams Lake, an organization with a mission to help support healthy communities. Marilyn is grateful to live in a country and community that welcomes and values diversity.

Tom Salley immigrated to Canada from the USA 40 years ago. He spends his time working on his organic farm, doing community/social work, and writing and performing his music.

Bettina Schoen emigrated from Germany to Canada in 1992 and has lived in the Cariboo ever since. Multiculturalism has been a strong interest and influence in Bettina's professional and personal life, and she enjoys managing the Multiculturalism Program at CMHA. She feels that *Spicing Up the Cariboo* is a unique project, bringing together a large diverse group of people in a simple way, through food and personal stories.